The Wizard's Craftbook

ANDREA WCISLEK

Magical DIY Crafts Inspired by Harry Potter,
Fantastic Beasts, The Lord of the Rings,
The Wizard of Oz, and More!

Skyhorse Publishing

Skyhorse Publishing books may be purchased in bulk at special discounts for sales promotion, corporate gifts, fund-raising, or educational purposes. Special editions can also be created to specifications. For details, contact the Special Sales Department, Skyhorse Publishing, 307 West 36th Street, 11th Floor, New York, NY 10018 or info@skyhorsepublishing.com.

Skyhorse® and Skyhorse Publishing® are registered trademarks of Skyhorse Publishing, Inc.®, a Delaware corporation.

Visit our website at www.skyhorsepublishing.com.

10 9 8 7 6 5 4 3 2 1

Library of Congress Cataloging-in-Publication Data is available on file.

Cover design by Mona Lin
Cover artwork credit: Andrea Wcislek
Interior artwork credit: Shutterstock; iStock; Andrea Wcislek

Print ISBN: 978-1-5107-4766-1
eBook ISBN: 978-1-5107-4767-8

Printed in China

Contents

Introduction

Who doesn't love fairy tales, Disney films, and the Harry Potter universe, and all of the whimsy and magic that comes along with them? Now with *The Wizard's Craftbook* you can bring some of that magic into your home! In this book you will find fifty magical crafts that range from movie-inspired prop replicas to fantastically geeky gifts and party decorations! With easy-to-follow instructions and step-by-step photos, you will find projects you can complete whether you are a beginner or an advanced crafter.

I created this book with a lot of love and magical inspiration. I have always enjoyed creating, whether it be art, photography, or crafts. About three years ago I decided to share my love of creating with the world through my YouTube channel, *Cooking and Craft Chick*. Sharing magical DIYs on my channel is what led me to create this book for you. I have included a few of the magical DIYs featured on my channel in this book, and I have included QR codes that can be scanned to take you to those videos so you can watch me create those crafts. Along with being able to see me make some of these crafts, you will notice that throughout this book you can also find QR codes that will take you to my website: https://cookingandcraftchi.wixsite.com/mysite to find free downloads of all the labels or templates used in my magical crafts. You will be able to use the crafts you create to customize a party, add a little magic to a room, or to give a very magical gift to any witch or wizard in your life! I hope you enjoy this book as much as I have enjoyed writing and designing it for you!

How to Scan a QR code

Whether you are using an Android or Apple IOS device you should be able to easily scan a QR code. First, open your camera app and steadily point it for two to three seconds towards the QR code you want to scan. Whenever scanning is enabled, a notification will appear; click on that notification and you will be immediately taken to the video or label. If nothing happens, you may have to go to your settings and enable QR code scanning. If scanning QR codes isn't an option in your settings, your device unfortunately can't scan QR codes natively. But don't worry, this only means you'll have to download a third-party QR code reader app from your app or play store.

Wrapping the Neck of Your Bottle

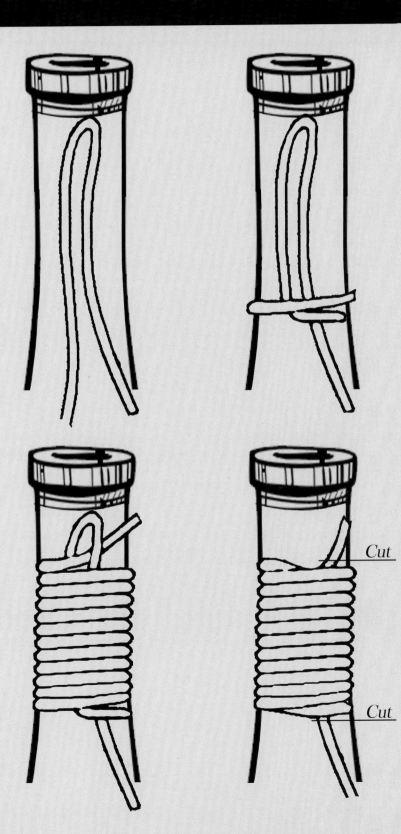

INSTRUCTIONS:

☆ Make a loop with your cord that goes above where you want the top of the wrapping to be.

☆ Then begin to wrap your cord around the bottle starting at the bottom and working your way up, encapsulating the loop.

☆ Once you have wrapped the whole neck of your bottle, put the end of your cording through the loop.

☆ Pull down on the bottom end of the cord (the bottom of the loop). This will pull the loop down and drag the end of your cord behind the wrap. This will knot it in place and you won't need any glue. Cut the top and bottom excess cord.

Cut

Cut

3

Beauty and the Beast
Enchanted Rose Cloche

Beauty and the Beast originated as a French fairytale, *La Belle et la Bête,* which has been rewritten and abridged for centuries, including two Disney versions. In both Disney movies, a beggar woman seeking refuge pleads with Prince Adam for shelter and offers him a rose for payment. Appalled that she would even ask this of him he refuses and turns the woman away. The beggar instantly transforms into a beautiful enchantress who had been testing his heart. Finding it to have no love, she punishes him by transforming him into a hideous Beast and leaving the enchanted rose which would bloom until his twenty-first birthday. If he learned to love and earn love in return before the last petal fell, the spell would be broken. Now you can have your very own Enchanted Rose, and unlike the Beast's, it will never wither away.

WHAT YOU WILL NEED:

- *Wooden base*
- *Silver paint and brush*
- *Glass cloche*
- *Zig® glue pen*
- *Iridescent glitter*
- *Strand of crystal beads*
- *1 large crystal bead*
- *1 loose smaller crystal bead*
- *Floral Pin with crystal head (or you can glue loose beads together without the pin.)*
- *Hot glue*
- *Hammer*
- *Nail*
- *Red silk rose*
- *Red silk rose petals*
- *Fairy lights*

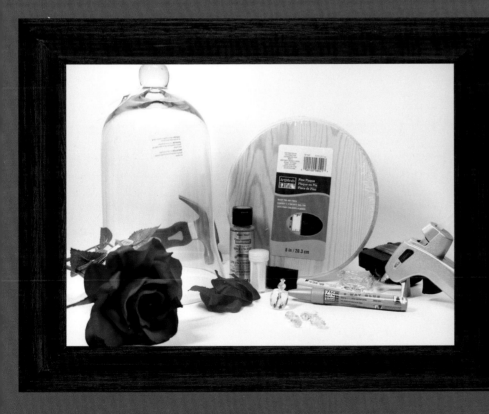

1. Start by taking the wood base and painting it silver with the silver acrylic paint.

2. While it dries, take your Zig glue pen and start to draw lines down the sides of the cloche, starting from the top. Make the lines mimic frozen frost lines. Once you have drawn the line, sprinkle the iridescent glitter over the glue line and then blow the excess away. This will leave you a magical icy line on the cloche. Continue to draw and glitter the lines around the whole top and bottom of the cloche. Be sure to vary the heights and shapes of the lines so it doesn't feel too patterned.

3. Once you have drawn and glittered all of the lines, take your strand of crystal beads and measure how many you will need to go around the neck of the cloche handle. Then, string and tie off the beads so that the knot is hidden and it gives a great glittery detail to the top of the cloche.

4. After you have strung the beads take your larger bead, smaller bead, and a rhinestone floral pin with crystal head, and hot glue them together. Once the hot glue has dried glue the combination to the top of the cloche handle.

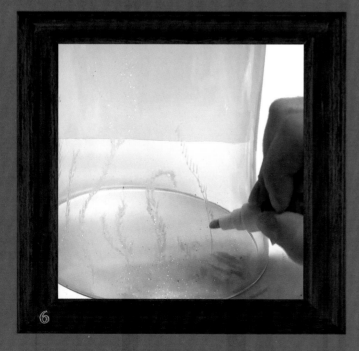

5. Now that your base has dried, find the center of the base and hammer a nail through the back so the nail is sticking through the top.

6. Then measure how tall you need your rose to be in the cloche and use scissors, pliers, or flower cutters to cut your rose to the right height. After your rose is cut to the right length use the nail to place the rose on the base. If your rose is tight enough on the nail you may not need to glue it. After your rose is placed, glue your silk petals in place to cover the base of the stem and to help fill in the base.

7. Then take your fairy string lights and glue them around the base of the cloche so they will shine through the glass. After this is complete place the cloche over the base and your Enchanted Rose Cloche is complete.

To see me make the Enchanted Rose Cloche scan this QR code!

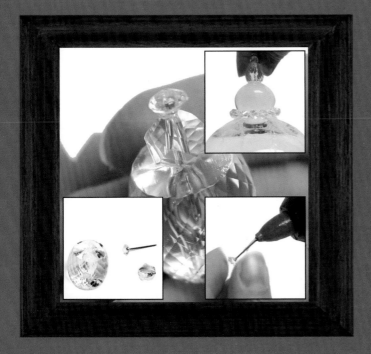

Beauty and the Beast
Enchanted Rose Bath Bomb

Just like the Enchanted Rose in Disney's *Beauty and the Beast* (1991) slowly withered away as the years passed, you can watch this rose wither away in your bathtub, and when it's done you are left with beautiful sparkly water that breaks the spell!

WHAT YOU WILL NEED:

- *Silicone rose mold (or plastic chocolate mold cleaned with rubbing alcohol)*

- *¼ cup cornstarch*

- *¼ cup citric acid*

- *½ cup baking soda*

- *¼ cup epsom salt*

- *1 tsp carrier oil (coconut, castor oil, and almond oil are best)*

- *½ tsp essential oil (I used a mix of rose and vanilla)*

- *½ tsp water*

- *Red food coloring or soap coloring (which will look pink)*

- *Bowl for mixing*

- *Whisk and spoon*

- *Gold body glitter*

1. After dumping all of the dry ingredients into the bowl, whisk them together. Continue mixing until all ingredients are well incorporated and there are no lumps.

2. Now mix the wet ingredients in a separate bowl.

3. Then SLOWLY add a drop or two of your wet ingredients into the dry ingredients, whisking the whole time. If you do not continually whisk and add the wet ingredients gradually, the wet will activate the dry ingredients, and your bath bomb will start to fizz instead of dry out.

4. Continue to combine the ingredients and continue mixing until it looks like fresh powdered snow. You should be able to pinch it and it should start to stick together. (If it feels too wet or sounds like it is fizzing, add more of your dry ingredients to balance it back out.)

5. Now add a little bit of the body glitter to the mixture so it will have some sparkle all the way through the bath bomb.

6. Prep your mold by adding some of the body glitter into the bottom. This will add a kiss of glitter to the edges of the petals.

7. Now start to scoop and press your mixture into the mold. Press the bath bomb mixture firmly into the mold with the back of a spoon.

8. Let your packed molds sit for at least four hours, if not overnight, before you start to unmold them. I find with the silicone molds the best way to unmold your bath bombs is to place a cutting board or other flat surface on top of your mold and flip all of it over and then lift your mold off.

9. You are then left with a lovely, fragrant Enchanted Rose Bath Bomb. When it is placed in the water it fizzes beautifully, leaving your water a magical pink color with some glitter floating on the top.

* These make a great gift — just place them in a plastic bag tied shut or in a little box!

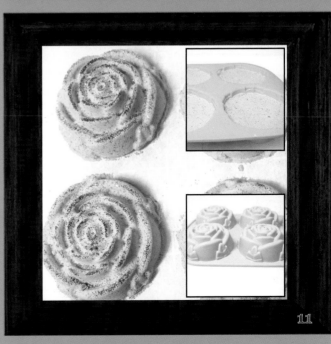

Yzma's Llama Potion

In Disney's *The Emperor's New Groove*, Yzma is an evil sorceress and the former advisor to Emperor Kuzco. After Kuzco fires Yzma, she decides to get revenge and murder Kuzco so she can become Empress. With the help of her assistant, Kronk, Yzma chooses to poison Kuzco with one of her numerous potions. Besides poisons, her potions can turn you into anything from animals to insects. Unfortunately, the llama potion's label rolled down and looked like a skull (the normal label for a poison), which is how Kronk accidentally turned Kuzco into a llama instead of killing him. Now you can have your own llama potion!

WHAT YOU WILL NEED:

- *3.5-oz. glass bottle with cork*

- *Funnel*

- *Rubbing alcohol*

- *Pink metallic acrylic paint (I used FolkArt's Color Shift® in Pink Flash)*

- *Your label printed on sticker paper, or regular paper and glue or Mod Podge®*

How to make it

1. Uncork your bottle and place your funnel inside, to make sure that your rubbing alcohol doesn't go everywhere.

2. Fill your bottle with the alcohol. I didn't fill mine all the way to make sure there was some room to shake the potion up to see the swirling effect we get.

3. Remove the funnel and take your metallic acrylic paint and add a decent amount to the bottle—however, not much is needed to fully color the alcohol. (I love the FolkArt Color Shift paints. They give amazing opalescent swirling inside the potion bottle.)

4. Re-cork your bottle, and shake it up until the paint is mixed in and you get a great swirling effect when the potion is shaken. (The mica powder that is in the metallic paint will eventually settle to the bottom of the bottle leaving a solid pink color; simply re-shake it to reactivate the mica to get the swirling effect again.)

5. Once your paint is thoroughly mixed into the alcohol, you can apply your potion label to the outside of the bottle. (If your bottle feels like it has a film, use some rubbing alcohol on a paper towel to clean the bottle.) If you are using sticker paper simply remove the backing paper and stick the label to the bottle. (On curved bottles you may need to use your nail or a credit card to rub the edges down thoroughly.) If you are not using sticker paper you can use regular paper and glue or Mod Podge to stick it to the bottle.

6. Once you have applied your label your bottle is complete. If your bottle will be around children you may want to glue the cork onto the bottle. I recommend using E6000 glue to glue the cork on.

15

Fantastic Beasts:
The Crimes of Grindelwald
Mooncalf Eye Drops

The Mooncalf is a shy magical creature that can only be seen during a full moon. They are known for their long necks and extremely large blue eyes. During a full moon they execute a complex dance on their hind legs creating what muggles call "crop circles."

These eye drops were created by Newt Scamander and are used to help cure any eye issues for the Mooncalves, which is really important because of the size of their eyes. Three drops of these eye drops are to be used on the Mooncalf nightly.

WHAT YOU WILL NEED:

- *Amber glass bottle with cork*
- *Metal turkey baster*
- *Rubbing alcohol*
- *Brown acrylic paint*
- *White metallic acrylic paint*
- *Bronze metallic acrylic paint*
- *Foam brush*
- *Label printed on sticker paper (or regular paper and glue)*
- *Jute twine*
- *Lighter (optional)*

How to make it

1. First, use your brown acrylic paint and dry sponge on your turkey baster to "age" it and make it appear more like leather. (I pushed the rubber part of the baster all the way down to slightly shorten the length of the baster and make it feel more like an eye dropper.) I added some metallic brown paint to the metal portion of the dropper as well.

2. While your dropper is drying, use your funnel to fill your bottle with rubbing alcohol. Leave some space at the top so it will shake up easier.

3. Then add some of the white or pearl acrylic paint to the bottle.

4. Re-cork your bottle and shake it up to thoroughly mix your paint into the alcohol. Once it is mixed it will give a great swirling effect. The mica in the paint will settle, but will re-swirl once it is shaken or stirred again.

5. Once your solution has been mixed up, you can add your label to the bottle. If you are using sticker paper, just remove the backing and place it wherever you want. (If you are not using sticker paper you can use regular paper and Mod Podge or regular glue.)

6. To give a more complex look you can wrap the neck of the bottle with jute twine. (See page 3, Wrapping the Neck of Your Bottle.)

7. (Optional) You can carefully use a lighter to "age" the twine. The lighter will remove any wispy cord pieces and slightly darken your twine.

 To download this Mooncalf Eye Drops Label scan this QR code!

 To see me make this Mooncalf Eye Drop Bottle scan this QR code!

19

Fantastic Beasts: The Crimes of Grindelwald
Skull Hookah

Made of an aged human skull, the Skull Hookah belonged to Gellert Grindelwald, one of the most powerful and dangerous Dark Wizards of all time, only being surpassed by Lord Voldemort. When used, it allowed others to experience Grindelwald's visions of the future. The text on the front of the skull includes the symbol of Gellert Grindelwald's army as well as the German inscription, "*Für das Größere Wohl*," which translates to "For the Greater Good."

WHAT YOU WILL NEED:

- *Skull replica that is not solid, preferably hollow where the brain would be (mine had a removable jaw, which was perfect)*

- *Removable vinyl (or copy paper and a pencil for a transfer technique)*

- *Black acrylic paint*

- *Cloth or foam brush*

- *Battery-operated LED rice lights*

- *Hot glue gun and glue*

- *Nylon cording (I went with a tan/white combo)*

- *Spring door stopper*

- *Krylon clear coat (optional)*

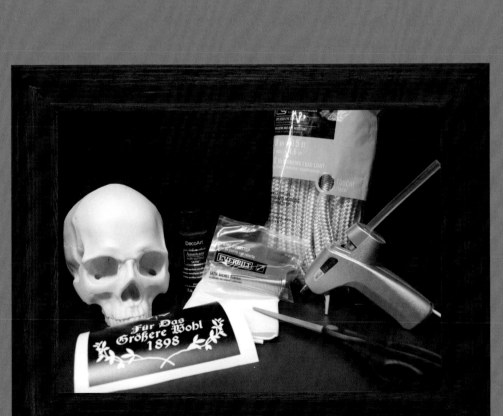

1. Start by cutting your vinyl on a Cricut® to create a stencil. If you don't have a Cricut you can use the paper/pencil transfer technique (like we used on our Encantus Spellbook, page 139).

2. Use transfer sheets or contact paper to apply your vinyl to the skull. (You may need to cut some slits in the surrounding vinyl so it contours to the skull better.) Really rub and press your vinyl down so no paint can seep under the edges.

3. Then remove your contact paper, leaving the vinyl stencil ready to use. Start to dab your black acrylic paint on with a cloth. Be sure to do a thinner coat so it doesn't bleed under the vinyl.

4. Once your black paint is the shade you want (I went with a lighter, more aged look), allow it to dry completely. Then carefully remove the vinyl from the skull. (You may need a weeding tool to remove some of the smaller pieces.)

5. Now we can load the lights into the cranium. Most hollow skulls have a small hole in the back or the bottom you can push the lights through. However, if your skull doesn't have a hole, carefully drill one. Once you have loaded all of your lights into the skull, add a drop of hot glue to hold them in place. (Your battery pack can either be held in your hand under the skull or set behind your skull.)

6. Next, measure out the length of the nylon or "hookah" cord and cut it. Because nylon is made of plastic you can carefully use a lighter or candle to melt the ends together so they won't fray and unravel. (You may want to use a pair of pliers to help push your cords together.)

7. Then take your spring door stopper and remove the rubber end and the back flat piece so you are left with just the spring. This is going to become the mouth piece for the cord. After your rope ends are melted glue one of the ends to the base of the skull, and the other end of the cord onto the end of the spring. (If you don't like how shiny the spring is you can "age" it by rubbing some brown or black acrylic paint on it.) Now your skull hookah is complete. Light it up and watch it glow!

*   This would be a great addition to a cosplay costume!

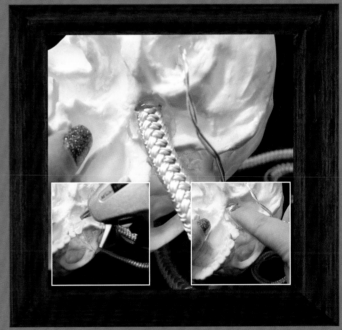

To download the Skull Design scan this QR code!

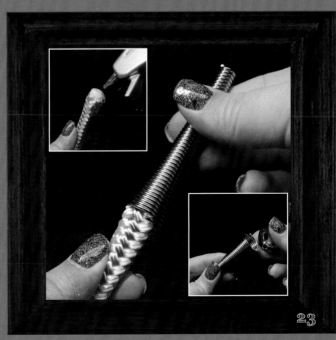

Fantastic Beasts and Where to Find Them
Occamy Eggshells

The Occamy is aggressive to all who approach it, particularly in defense of its eggs, which are made of the purest, softest silver. Because of this, the shells are quite valuable and may be used as an ingredient in potions, such as the Felix Felicis potion. This is a tutorial of how to create silver Occamy Eggshells that look like they came straight out of Newt Scamander's case!

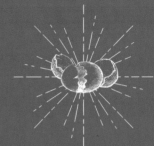

WHAT YOU WILL NEED:

- *Papier-mâché eggs (the eggs I used are 4" x 2.5")*

- *Box cutter or X-ACTO® knife (please be careful!)*

- *Silver acrylic paint*

- *Pearl white acrylic paint*

- *Glossy and matte Mod Podge®*

- *Silver glitter*

- *Paintbrushes*

- *Silver leaf or silver leaf flakes*

- *Silver paint marker*

1. Carefully use your X-ACTO knife and cut around the center of the egg to make it look broken.

2. Once your egg is cut open paint the inside with your silver acrylic paint. This will create a base for our silver leafing we will apply later.

3. While waiting for the inside of the egg to dry, paint the outside with the pearl white acrylic paint.

4. Allow the outside of the egg to dry, and then mix your matte finish Mod Podge with the silver glitter.

5. Paint your Mod Podge mix over the entire outside of the egg. The Mod Podge will dry clear so you will be left with the glitter over your pearl paint giving a luster effect.

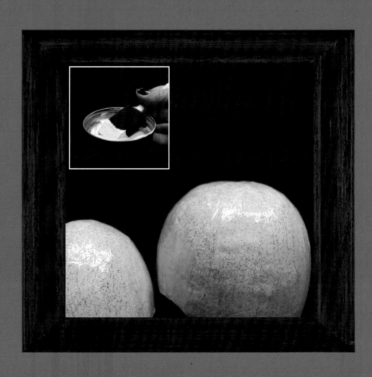

6. Once the outside of the egg is completely dry, turn it over and paint the inside of the egg with glossy Mod Podge. Wait two to five minutes until the glue is tacky, but not dry. Dump some of the silver leaf flakes into the egg. Use a dry paintbrush to press the flakes all over the inside of the egg. Allow it to dry completely.

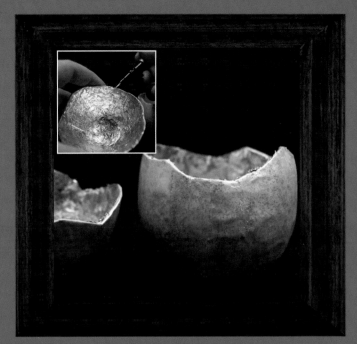

7. After the glue holding the flakes has dried, use the dry paintbrush to knock off any excess flakes and smooth out your silver finish.

8. Paint a coat of the glossy Mod Podge over the silver leaf to seal it. Again, the Mod Podge dries clear so the beauty of the silver leafing will shine through.

9. Finally, use a silver paint marker (or carefully use silver paint) to go around the edge of the egg to give it a clean seamless look.

To see me make these Occamy Eggshells scan this QR code!

Fantastic Beasts and Where to Find Them
Swooping Evil Venom

The Swooping Evil is a blue-and-green, winged magical creature. When it is not flying it shrinks into a spiny cocoon. While in cocoon form it is able to secrete a venom that, when properly diluted, can be used to erase bad memories. A test tube of the venom was delivered across New York City through a rainstorm created by a Thunderbird named Frank, performing a Memory Charm over the city's entire No-Maj population and preserving the secrecy and security of the magical community. This venom also has a magical property that makes it glow!

WHAT YOU WILL NEED:

- *Plaid Glo-Away® glowing gel paint*

- *Mixing cup*

- *Neon blue acrylic paint*

- *Spoon*

- *Glass test tube with cork*

- *Funnel (optional)*

- *Skewer (if using a funnel)*

- *Venom label printed on sticker paper (or regular paper and glue)*

1. First take your Plaid Glow-Away glow-in-the-dark gel—which, after lots of testing, was the best medium, with the best glow—and place it in your mixing cup.

2. Then add your neon blue acrylic paint to the glow gel.

3. Mix the two together with a spoon until you get your desired color. It's always better to start with just a little bit of paint and keep adding to get your color, rather than making it too dark.

4. Use a funnel (or piping bag) to add your solution to the test tube. If you have trouble getting the solution in, use a cooking skewer. (After making this, if I was doing it again, I would use a piping bag verses the funnel.)

5. Once your test tube is filled remove the funnel.

6. Re-cork your test tube, being sure to push it in as far as it will go. (If you would like to glue the cork on, I recommend E-6000 glue.)

7. Then, take your label printed on either sticker paper (or regular paper and glue) and place it on the test tube.

8. Once your label is on your test tube, apply your test tube to some light and turn the lights off and watch it glow!

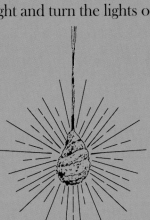

 To download of the Swooping Evil Venom Label, scan this QR code. Or visit: https://cookingandcraftchi. wixsite.com/mysite

 To see me make Swooping Evil Venom scan this QR code!

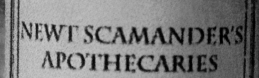

NEWT SCAMANDER'S
APOTHECARIES

~ London, England ~

ERUMPENT
MUSK

CAUTION: USE JUST A FEW DROPS
TO ATTRACT FEMALES OF THE
ERUMPENT SPECIES
VERY POWERFUL

Fantastic Beasts and Where to Find Them
Erumpent Musk

The Erumpent is a huge African magical beast which resembles a rhinoceros. Its horn, which can pierce almost anything, contains a fluid that explodes, destroying what it has hit. Because male Erumpents frequently blow each other up during mating season, the species is somewhat endangered—this is why Erumpent Musk is so important. Erumpent musk is a liquid obtained from male Erumpents that, along with a mating dance, attracts females of the species. Be careful with this bottle of musk—you may have more than you bargained for if some of the musk spills out and a female Erumpent is nearby!

WHAT YOU WILL NEED:

- *Glass bottle*
- *Sandpaper*
- *Green dish soap or other green shelf-stable liquid*
- *Potion label printed on sticker paper (or regular paper and glue)*

How to make it

1. Take your glass bottle and rub your sandpaper in all different directions to give your bottle a more aged look.

2. Once your bottle appears aged, fill it with a shelf-stable green liquid. I like to use a green dish soap.

3. Re-cork your glass bottle, being sure to push it in as far as it will go. (If you would like to glue the cork on, I recommend E-6000 glue.)

4. Then, take your label printed on either sticker paper (or regular paper and glue) and place it on the bottle.

Free download of the Erumpent Musk Label.Or visit: https://cookingandcraftchi.wixsite.com/mysite

To see me make this Erumpent Musk scan this QR code!

34

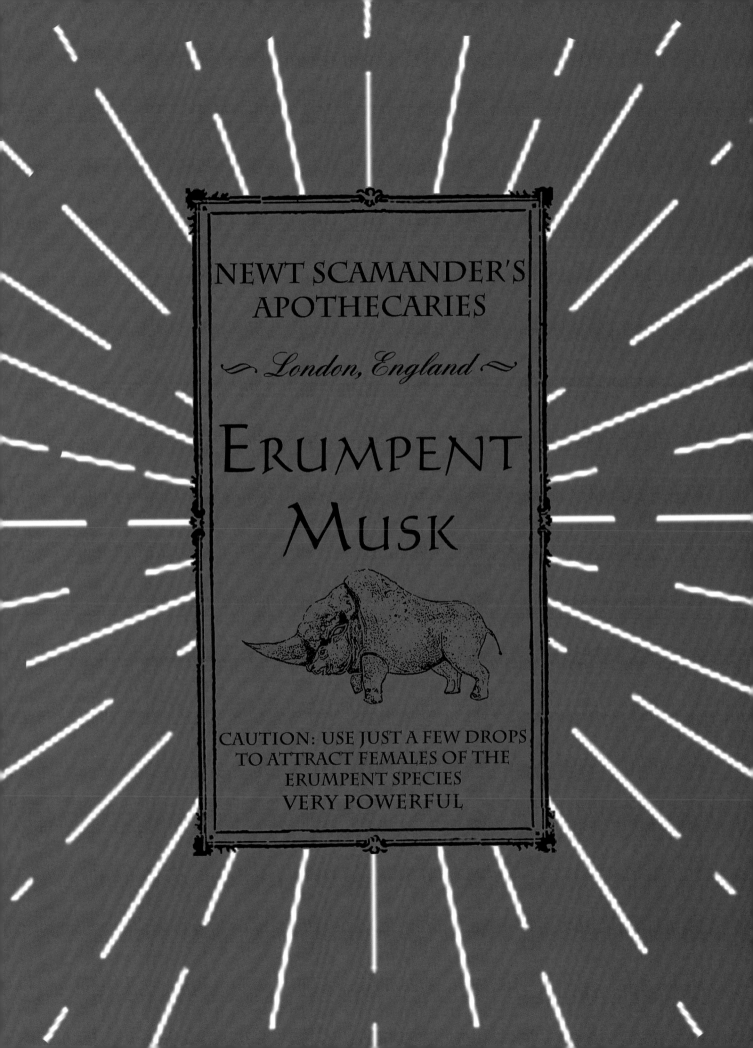

Game of Thrones
Rhaegal's Dragon Egg

Daenerys Targaryen is given three petrified dragon eggs as a gift for her wedding to Khal Drogo. The three eggs are black/red, green, and gold. Daenerys experiments with her eggs to try to get them to hatch. Finally, after several failed attempts, she is found in the remnants of a giant pyre with the three newly-hatched baby dragons: a black dragon, Drogon, clinging to her shoulder; a green dragon, Rhaegal, in her arms; and a white dragon, Viserion, clinging to her leg. This is a copy of Rhaegal's Dragon Egg.

WHAT YOU WILL NEED:

- *Papier-mâché egg*

- *Black adhesive foam craft sheets (I used two sheets)*

- *Scissors or a Cricut® cutter*

- *Acrylic paint in metallic green, metallic bronze, and gold*

- *Foam brush*

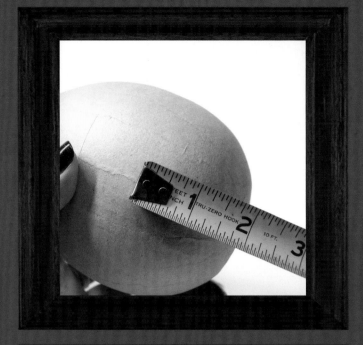

1. First, take your papier-mâché egg and, measuring up a couple of inches from the bottom, draw a line to know where to start placing your scales. (To help make it easier to draw a line use a rubber band as a guide.)

2. Then either hand-cut your scale strips out of the adhesive craft foam (see QR code for a scales template) or have a Cricut cut them for you. (Make sure to change the material setting to heavy craft foam so it cuts properly.) You will need two full sheets of the scales to completely fill your egg. It is important that you use the adhesive foam or you will have to glue every strip of the craft foam. (If you are hand-cutting your scales, print the template on sticker paper. Then adhere it to the back of your adhesive foam sheet. This will make it much easier to cut accurately.)

3. Start by placing your scale strip across the line you created on the egg. After your first row is complete, stagger the second row so the scales are not in a perfectly aligned row. Continue placing the scales all the way up the egg. Be sure to press the scales down thoroughly to make sure you get full adhesion.

4. Once you get to the very top of the egg, use the slightly smaller scales on the sheet. Then place the 4-point scale on the egg and finish it with the circle.

5. Now that you have completely covered the egg you can start to paint it. For the first layer start with your green paint darkened by bronze paint. After the first layer has dried paint a lighter layer on top.

6. When you have your desired color achieved, paint the bottom of the egg in the lighter green shade. Once that has dried take your gold paint and dry brush the entire bottom of the egg. This will give the bottom a textured look.

7. Then dry brush the entire egg with the gold paint, adding complexity to the scales. Allow to dry completely and prepare to hatch your dragon egg!

 For a Dragon Scales template scan this QR code!

Harry Potter
Wands

A wand is a magical instrument through which a witch or wizard channels her or his magical powers to concentrate the effects for more precise results. Wands are most notably made by famous wandmaker Ollivander in Great Britain and Gregorovitch in Eastern Europe. Each wand consists of a wand-quality wood that surrounds a core of magical substance, such as unicorn hair, dragon heartstring, etc. Now you can make your own wands—just remember that no two wands are ever alike!

WHAT YOU WILL NEED:

- *10.6" (27cm) large bamboo chopstick*

- *Hot glue gun and glue (you may want to use colored glue sticks too)*

- *Beads*

- *Wire*

- *Twine*

- *Acrylic paints in various shades*

- *Whatever you want to add to your wand!*

1. First, you need to decide the "core" of your wand; I used a larger bamboo chopstick. They are 10.6" long and are more round than square.

2. Next, you need to decide how many and what style of wands you want to make. Do you want to have a textured wand, a sleek wand, a fancy bead at the end, etc.?

3. Once you decide on the wand style, gather the supplies you want for that wand and use your hot glue gun to start to build up the wand, or to add designs. You can give your wand a more woody effect or add texture by gluing on little beads. Or you can add rope to make a different type of handle, wire in swirls, etc.

4. After you have your wand base started you can then paint your wand. You may decide to go with a more traditional look of wood tones, or you can add metallic paints, or anything you want—it's completely customizable. Just be sure that all of your hot glue is completely cool before starting to paint.

5. I like to do several different coats of paint; I may paint the base a solid brown, and then go over the details with a metallic paint like gold or silver. You can also use colored hot glues, or paint markers over regular hot glue, to give a unique look to your wand.

6. After your wands are complete and the way you would like them, you may want to spray them with a Krylon clear coat to protect the finishes you placed on the wand.

* These wands make a great favor at a party, or a fun activity to do with older kids!

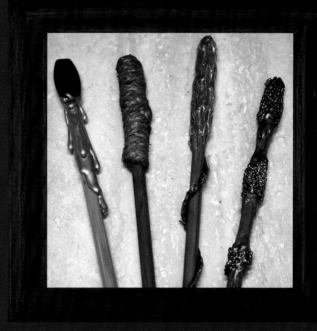

Amortentia

Amortentia is the most powerful love potion in existence. When brewed properly it gives off an aroma that smells differently to each person. It smells of whatever they find most attractive, even if they are unaware of the affection themselves; because of this it's considered highly dangerous. Despite its power, Amortentia doesn't create actual love—that would be impossible—but it does create a strong infatuation, or obsession. Because of the strong effects of this potion, it may be the most dangerous potion on your shelf!

WHAT YOU WILL NEED:

- *Heart bottle with cork*

- *Clear alcohol-free thick styling gel*

- *Piping bag (or sandwich bag) for filling*

- *Red food coloring*

- *Gold and red glitter*

- *Your label printed on sticker paper (or regular paper and glue or Mod Podge®)*

- *Glittery tulle to embellish (optional)*

- *Red twine (optional)*

1. Place your piping bag or sandwich bag inside a cup or vase and fill it with a decent amount of hair gel—enough to fill your bottle all the way up.

2. Then add your food coloring to the gel. Mix thoroughly, being sure to fold the gel all the way to the bottom to make sure all of the gel is the same color.

3. Once you have your desired color, mix the gold and red glitter into the gel until you get your desired consistency.

4. Take your piping bag and squeeze all of the gel to the bottom, then snip the end so you can fill your bottle. Place the piping bag into the uncorked bottle and fill it to the top with your colored gel. You may need to tap your bottle on the table to release any air bubbles.

5. Once your bottle is filled, recork it. Now, you can apply your potion label to the outside of the bottle. (If your bottle feels like it has a film, use some rubbing alcohol on a paper towel to clean the bottle.) If you are using sticker paper simply remove the backing paper and stick the label to the bottle. (On curved bottles you may need to use your nail or a credit card to rub the edges down thoroughly.) If you are not using sticker paper you can use regular paper and glue or Mod Podge to stick it to the bottle.

6. Once you have applied your label to your bottle, you can embellish it further by cutting a square of glittery tulle and tying it onto the neck of the bottle with the red cording. Then unwind the ends of your cording to mimic a tassel effect. Your bottle is then complete.

 To download the Potion Label scan this QR code!

 To see me make Amortentia Love Potion scan this QR code!

Magic can be performed with more than just a wand.....

Feather Quill Ink Pen

A quill pen is a writing implement made from a molted primary wing feather of a large bird. While quills were most used in the sixth through nineteenth centuries, before the invention of the metal dip pen and later ballpoint pens, it is still the preferred method of writing among witches and wizards. This Quill Pen is a great melding of a traditional-looking quill with the convenience of a ballpoint pen. Now you can write with a quill without the mess and hassle of dipping your quill into ink!

WHAT YOU WILL NEED:

- Larger feathers

- Ink pens (non-click style)

- Scissors

- A cooking skewer or stick to help prep the feather if the ink doesn't go in easily.

- Hot glue gun and glue

1. Select your feather, making sure that it is large enough to hold the ink tube and feels comfortable in your hand.

2. Snip the very end of the feather off with your scissors.

3. Take your ballpoint pen apart so you are left with just the ink tube.

4. Once you have your hollow feather tip you can push your ink into the shaft of the feather. If you have trouble use your cooking skewer or stick to "pre-bore" the feather to fit the ink.

5. The ink should barely move once in the feather. If it does use the hot glue gun to tightly secure it.

6. Allow your hot glue to dry completely and make sure your ink tube does not move or pull out of the feather.

7. Now you can write easily without having to dip your feather into ink.

* These are great for a party as well as for kids.

* If the back of your feather cracks while you are inserting your ink, just seal it with your hot glue. Then use a matching color permanent marker over the glue to camouflage it. (If your feather is white a white paint marker will cover your glue.) Most feathers will not crack unless they are too small.

Harry Potter

Prophecy

A Prophecy comes into existence when a Seer begins reciting a prophecy involuntarily. They often appear to have entered a trance-like state while giving the prophecy sometimes in an altered voice. As is the case with Sybill Trelawney, the Seer doesn't seem to remember the event, and is left exhausted.

A Prophecy is recorded in a spun-glass, orb-shaped object. The orbs are kept in the Hall of Prophecies inside the Department of Mysteries in the Ministry of Magic in London. The prophecy orb can only be removed from the Hall by those mentioned in the Prophecy.

WHAT YOU WILL NEED:

- *Opalescent glass ornament bulb (I used a 4" bulb)*

- *Rubbing alcohol in a spray bottle*

- *Krylon Looking Glass® spray paint*

- *Heat gun or hair dryer (optional)*

- *LED tea light (I used a cool white light tea light)*

- *Teal permanent marker*

- *Fiber fill or pillow stuffing*

- *Base to hold your prophecy (napkin rings, votive cups, etc. work well. I used a paper clip holder from the dollar store)*

1. Begin by removing the metal top of your ornament. Then spritz the inside of the bulb with the rubbing alcohol (one to two sprays is plenty). The alcohol helps give a mercury glass effect and adds more design.

2. Then spray the Looking Glass spray on the inside of the bulb. Roll the bulb so the paint hits every inch of the inside.

3. If you want to speed up the drying process, especially between coats, take a hair dryer or heat gun and carefully blow into the bulb. (Do not overheat your glass, and be careful not to burn yourself; the glass heats up quickly.)

4. Once your first coat has dried, I recommend spraying a second coat. The Looking Glass spray won't look like much until it fully dries, then it gives an amazing mirror-like, mercury glass look to the bulb.

5. While your bulb dries completely, take your **LED** tea light and begin to color the flame, or light portion, with your permanent marker. This will change the color of the light from white to teal.

6. Then stuff some fiber fill or pillow stuffing into the inside of your bulb. This will help diffuse the light and give more of a "misty" look to the inside of the Prophecy.

7. Then you can insert your **LED** light to illuminate your bulb. Depending on your base, you may decide to glue your light into place (I didn't find this to be necessary for mine).

8. Finally, place your prophecy and light on top of your chosen base.

 To download a Prophecy Tag scan this QR code!

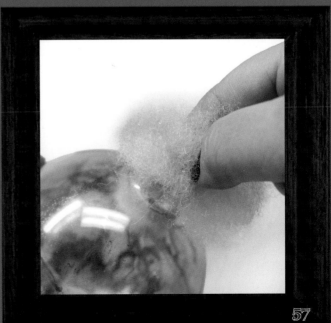

Harry Potter
Butterbeer Candle

Butterbeer is the quintessential wizard drink described by J. K. Rowling as tasting "a little bit like a less-sickly butterscotch."* It is served warm and foaming in tankards or chilled in bottles and can be found in wizard pubs such as The Three Broomsticks or The Hog's Head. This candle embodies the smell and look of a Butterbeer, including the iconic frothy foam!

WHAT YOU WILL NEED:

- Paraffin wax

- Heat-resistant measuring cup

- Glass mug

- Wick

- Glue dots

- Candle coloring, or bits of crayons or old candles to color (I used caramel coloring)

- Fragrance oil or essential oil (I used butter toffee crème brûlée oil for the body and vanilla for the cream)

- Skewers or a wick holder

- Metal spatula

- Clear plastic fork

- Piping bag or plastic sandwich bag

---

* Rowling, J. K. Interview. *Bon Appétit* magazine, 2002.

1. Start by placing your paraffin wax into a heat resistant measuring cup. Heat your paraffin wax in the microwave in thirty-second intervals, stirring after each interval until the wax is melted. (Do this carefully! Wax can catch fire if overheated.) You could also use a double boiler method to heat.

2. To insert the wick into the glass mug, place your wick into a straw and stick a glue dot onto the bottom. Then use the straw to guide the wick into the bottom of the glass mug. Once attached, you can remove the straw.

3. Once your wax is melted use your candle coloring to slowly darken your wax. Please note that your wax will appear much darker than it will when it is cooled. To test the color place a small dot of the wax onto some parchment paper and let it dry to know that you have the desired color. Then add your fragrance until you feel you have the right strength.

4. Once you have the perfect color and fragrance fill your glass container and then use the skewers or a wick holder to ensure that your wick is in the center of the mug.

5. While your candle is cooling melt a small amount of wax and add fragrance if desired.

6. Then use your spatula to stir the wax to help it start to cool. Once it starts to cool and become opaque change your stirring tool to a plastic fork. The fork will keep the mixture from clumping while it cools. Keep stirring until your wax gets to the consistency of whipped cream or frosting. You want to be able to pull your fork up and have the wax form a peak as it is pulled out.

7. Once your wax is "whipped cream" consistency, take a piping bag or plastic sandwich bag and place it inside a glass to hold it in place. Then fill the piping bag with the wax.

8. Snip the corner of the piping bag and pipe your wax onto the top of the candle, being careful to keep the wick in the center. (You can add a piping tip if you want your foam to look really uniform but I liked the more "rustic" look.) Allow your candle to cool completely overnight, and cut the wick to ¼" before burning it.

* This yielded enough wax to make two Butterbeer Candles.

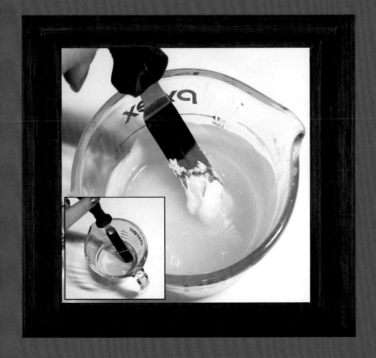

OWL POST SERVICE

Please Feed Owl Upon Delivery

CHARMED
HANDLE WITH CARE!

PACKED
BY
HOUSE ELVES

Mr. H. Potter
The Cupboard under the Stair
4. Privet Drive
Little Whinging.
SURREY

on Delivery

Owl Post Packages

Owl Post is the main method of sending and receiving messages or items using owls as the carriers. Wizards either tie messages or parcels to the owls' legs or have the owls carry the parcel in their beaks. Considered by wizards to be "the normal way" of communicating, owl post functions in a manner similar to muggle post, complete with post offices. These packages are adorned with labels, stickers, wax seals, and wrappings similar to any package you may find in the wizarding world. These will make a perfect gift wrap or a fun way to send muggle post to your favorite wizard! Just don't forget to feed the owl upon delivery.

WHAT YOU WILL NEED:

- *Gift or package you wish to wrap*

- *Tape*

- *Scissors*

- *Brown parcel paper*

- *Twine, string, or ribbon*

- *Your stickers and labels printed on sticker paper (or regular paper and glue)*

- *Wax seal stamp (optional)*

- *Hot glue gun (optional)*

- *Colored hot glue (optional)*

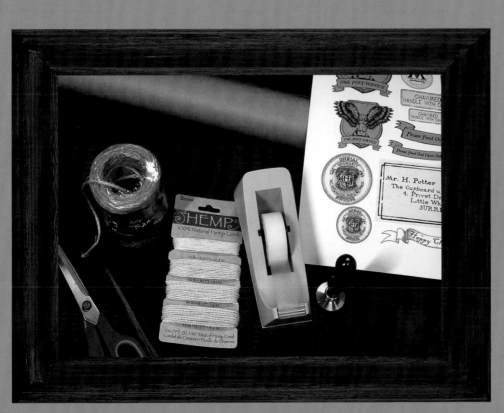

How to make it

1. Select your gift or package you wish to make magical and measure out your brown parcel paper. Grab your tape and scissors and wrap your gift or package with the brown parcel paper.

2. If desired, tie some string, jute twine, cording, or ribbon around your package.

3. To give your package a unique and fun look, use a hot glue gun with colored hot glue to create a wax seal. (You will find that if you are going to ship this package the hot glue is more pliable and won't crack and potentially break like true sealing wax sometimes can.)

4. Press your wax stamp into the warm hot glue—don't let cool until the stamp is in place.

5. Allow your hot glue to completely dry before removing your wax stamp. (If you don't have a wax seal you can use a coin or button to create a faux seal.)

6. Adorn your package with your stickers (don't forget about the sides and bottom). However, if you are going to use muggle post be sure to leave space for the postage.

7. Place your mailing label on the box (or use a Harry Potter label). If you are not mailing this through muggle post and it is a gift, you can just make out a To and From label.

8. Now you can mail your Owl Post Packages or have your owl leave them on a friend's front porch!

*   A fun tip: Use a brown lidded gift box so that your Owl Post Package can be re-used!

 To download the Owl Post stickers scan this QR code!

 To see me make these Owl Post Packages scan this QR code!

Harry Potter
Wizard Crackers

A Wizard Cracker is the wizarding variation of the common-ly known Christmas Cracker, which is a party favor given out at Christmas in the United Kingdom. Inside the Muggle crackers are prizes like a paper hat, a plastic toy, and a slip of paper with a joke printed on it. In order to get the prizes out, two people each hold one end of the cracker and pull it apart. The split is accompanied by a crack or snap (which is why they are called crackers). Wizard crackers go off with a bang as loud as a cannon blast, enveloping everyone nearby in a cloud of blue smoke. They contain the same hat, gift, and joke as the muggle variety, but the hats are real, and the gifts are extremely unique, even peculiar.

WHAT YOU WILL NEED:

- *Cardboard tubes (recycled toilet paper tubes)*

- *Scissors*

- *Tape*

- *Cracker snaps (a thin strip of chemically-infused cardboard for party poppers. Can be found online at Etsy.com.)*

- *Gold wrapping paper (be sure not to use foil paper; you want it to be able to tear)*

- *Ribbon*

- *Confetti*

- *Paper crown*

- *Joke*

- *Little gifts or candy*

- *House crests printed on sticker paper or regular paper and glue*

1. Take your cardboard tube and cut it in half. Once in half take your cracker snap and tape it down (or hot glue it—it needs to be stuck down really well) to the inside of the tube so the center snap section is in the middle.

2. After your snap is in place, cut your gold wrapping paper to just a little longer than your tube and just wide enough to wrap it completely.

3. Be sure when you wrap your tube that you tape your paper down on the two halves not in the center. You want to make sure that your cracker will pull apart.

4. After your tube is wrapped, take another cardboard tube and cut it in half. Insert the halves into the ends of the wrapping paper, leaving a gap between them and your cracker tube. (This gives a gap that will allow you to cleanly crimp and twist your paper giving you an area to tie.)

5. After you have twisted one side tie it with your ribbon. With one side tied insert your crown, joke, and trinkets or candy, and confetti (which will need to be large or it will fall out).

6. After the cracker is filled with the prizes crimp and twist the second end and tie on another ribbon. After both sides are tied shut remove the extra cardboard tube halves.

7. Now you can decorate it with a house crest sticker. (I made all of my crackers house themed and inserted a house themed button, and used ribbon and stickers to complete the look.)

8. Finally, pull your cracker apart, hear the great snap, and reveal the goodies inside!

To download the House Crest Stickers scan this QR code!

GILLYWEED

Gillyweed is a Magical plant native
to the Mediteranean Sea. When it
is eaten by a witch or wizard, one
grows gills and webbing between
the fingers and toes, allowing them
to process oxygen from ater and
navigate underwater more easily.

Harry Potter

Gillyweed Bottle

Gillyweed is a magical plant that is native to the Mediterranean Sea. When eaten, it gives humans fish-like properties, including gills to breathe under water, and webbing between the fingers and toes for easier swimming. There is some debate among herbologists as to the duration of the effects of gillyweed in fresh water versus salt water, but in fresh water, a sprig of gillyweed seems to last for about an hour. Now you can have your own supply of gillyweed!

WHAT YOU WILL NEED:

- *Glass bottle*

- *Moss, silk greens (seaweed-looking greens)*

- *Cooking skewer*

- *Green dish soap*

- *Label printed on sticker paper (or regular paper and glue)*

- *Jute twine (optional)*

- *Green grass wrap (optional)*

1. First, take your glass bottle and your silk leaf pieces and start to fill your bottle with the greens, berries, etc.

2. Once your bottle has a decent amount of the greens inside add a similar amount of moss. Use a cooking skewer to help position the moss inside the bottle. Then add more greens until you are happy with the look of the bottle.

3. Fill your bottle with green dish soap. (Note that most moss has been dyed, and it may deepen the green of your soap over time. You can use clear soap if you want a lighter green color.)

4. Once your bottle is completely filled use the cooking skewer to make sure everything is positioned how you would like. Once you are satisfied with the positioning re-cork your bottle.

5. Once your bottle is re-corked stick or glue your label onto the bottle.

6. To give a more complex look you can wrap the neck of the bottle with jute twine. (See page 3, Wrapping the Neck of Your Bottle.)

7. To add even more embellishment, add some of your greenery to the twine wrap, as well as some green grass ribbon.

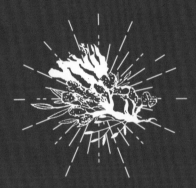

Free download of the Gillyweed Bottle label. Or visit: https://cookingandcraftchi.wixsite.com/mysite

To see me make this Gillyweed Bottle scan this QR code!

Harry Potter
Cauldron Stack

Potage's Cauldron Shop, owned by Madam Potage, is the first shop one encounters when entering Diagon Alley. It sells all types of cauldrons and displays them in a stack outside the shop. Now you can make a Cauldron Stack like the one you would find outside Potage's. Because we use a foam tape to help them stack, they can be stacked in any height or any order easily. Be sure to make a size two pewter cauldron since it is required for potions class for all first years.

WHAT YOU WILL NEED:

- *Assorted plastic cauldrons (I used a 16", a 12", an 11", a 10", two 8", and a 6" cauldron)*

- *Hot glue gun and glue*

- *Assorted spray paints (I used stone, flat black, black hammered metal, silver, and bronze spray paints. Be sure your spray paints will adhere to plastic; I recommend Krylon® brand)*

- *Marine and auto weather stripping, or other foam weather stripping or tape.*

- *Clear coat (optional. I recommend Krylon® brand.)*

1. Spread your cauldrons out and decide what colors and finishes you want to apply to each cauldron so you have a diverse-looking stack. If any of them have moveable handles, I recommend hot gluing them in place against the cauldron before painting it.

2. Once you've decided what color each cauldron will be, spray any that will receive a "stone" texture first. This is so it has time to dry before receiving its actual color. (You can spray the whole cauldron with the texture or just the top portion to create a sort of ombre effect.)

3. Continue to spray paint each cauldron with its assigned color. Some cauldrons may require two coats for full coverage. Be sure to let your cauldrons dry completely before you move onto the next step.

4. Your weather stripping usually comes as two tubes attached together. Separate the tubes so you have a single strip of the weather stripping. (This will also give you twice as much tape.)

5. Once your weather striping is separated wrap the tape around the inside rim to measure the length and cut it before removing the backing. (When in doubt cut it a little longer; you can always trim more if necessary.)

6. Remove the backing as you press the weather stripping to the inside rim of the cauldron. This will give a little resistance and cushion to the inside rim that will allow you to stack your cauldrons more easily, as well as be able to tilt them back and forth. This will also allow you to unstack your cauldrons for easier storage as well as help you customize your stack.

* If you want your stack to be a more permanent instillation you could hot glue the cauldrons together, or use silicone to adhere them in place.

* If you are going to stack this outside and it's windy you can add weight to each cauldron so it will stay in place without blowing over.

* Feel free to clear coat your cauldrons to protect their new finishes.

 To see me make this Cauldron Stack scan this QR code!

Harry Potter
Mandrake Pot

A mandrake is a plant which has a root that looks, when young, like a human baby but matures as the plant grows. Whenever unearthed, the root screams. Though a mature mandrake's scream will kill any person who hears it, a young mandrake's screams will usually only knock a person out for several hours. When herbology students study mandrakes, Professor Sprout has them wear earmuffs to protect themselves from the cries. Now you can have a pot to place your own mandrake plant in—just be sure to wear your earmuffs!

WHAT YOU WILL NEED:

- *Terracotta flower pot*

- *Removable vinyl cut into a stencil, (or you can use copy paper and a pencil for a transfer technique)*

- *Black acrylic paint*

- *Cloth or foam brush*

- *Plant*

- *Krylon® clear coat matte finish (optional)*

- *Fake moss (optional)*

How to make it

1. Start by cutting your vinyl on a Cricut® to create a stencil. If you don't have a Cricut you can use the paper/pencil transfer technique (like we used on our Encantus Spellbook, page 139).

2. Then use transfer or contact paper to apply your vinyl, and be sure to rub it on really well, especially around the edges, so the paint doesn't bleed under the vinyl when applying. Remove the transfer paper and your stencil should be perfectly applied.

3. Take your black acrylic paint and, with a cloth, dab the paint onto your stencil. Be careful to do a thin coat so your paint doesn't seep under the stencil.

4. After your first coat of paint you may decide to do a second coat to get a bolder color. However, you may like the lighter look of just one coat of paint.

5. Once your paint has completely dried you can peel your stencil off carefully. (You may need a weeding tool to pull off any smaller pieces of vinyl.)

6. After you have peeled your stencil you may want to spray your pot with a matte finish Krylon clear coat to protect your design from water and the elements. (If you decide to make this pot an outdoor pot, I would paint it with outdoor acrylic paint and clear coat it to give it extra protection from the elements.)

7. Finally, place (or plant) your plant in your pot. I used a Money Tree, or a Brussel's Bonsai, because it has a great woody base that branches off into great leaves. Other species of bonsai plants resemble a mandrake plant as well.

* I topped my pot off with some moss because Bonsai prefer to stay moist rather than the soil being wet, and the moss assists with that.

 To download this Mandrake Pot design scan this QR code!

Flying Keys Art

The Charms Professor, Filius Flitwick, enchanted a flock of Flying Keys with a flying charm to help guard the Sorcerer's Stone. Only one of the Flying Keys would allow entry into the following chamber through a locked door that was impervious to all charms. Brooms were provided to allow access to the keys, though the keys scattered chaotically as soon as the brooms took off. Now you can create a three-dimensional art piece, cards, etc. with magical flying keys!

WHAT YOU WILL NEED:

- *Flying Key wings printed on clear transfer paper, or overhead projector sheets*

- *Scissors*

- *Hot glue gun and glue*

- *Key sculpture or scrapbook metal key art with adhesive backs*

- *Picture frame, shadow box, mirror, card, etc. to place your keys on.*

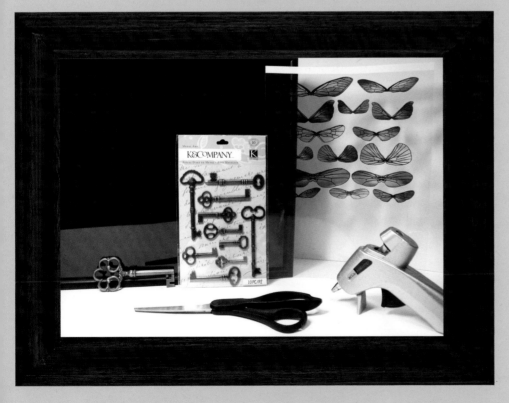

How to make it

1. Start by printing the Flying Key design onto clear overhead projector paper. Then cut each set of wings out. If you have a Cricut® you can use it to cut the wings out for you.

2. Once the wings are all cut, start to fold them in half so they appear to be more realistic. You can stagger the wings so they have movement, rather than folding them completely in half.

3. After all of your wings are ready, use your hot glue gun to place a dot of glue at the fold of the wings and attach it to the key.

4. If you glue the wings to a key sculpture, you can tie some fishing line to it so it appears to be flying. If you want to make a unique piece of art or decorate a mirror for a party, or make a unique card, you can use the scrapbooking metal adhesive keys like I did for the shadowbox.

5. Now you can stick the key to whatever surface you want to make more magical. Once you have placed your keys you will have a magical piece of art that seems to be flying off of the glass.

 To download the Flying Key Wings design, scan this QR code!

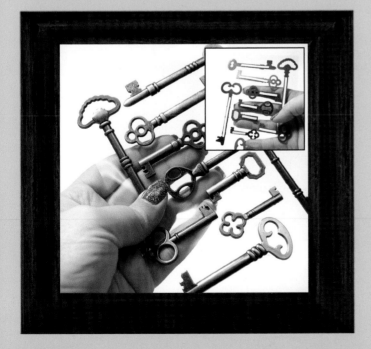

Harry Potter

Troll Bogies Slime

Bogies is the British term for "boogers." During the Halloween banquet of Harry Potter's first year, Professor Quirrell let a troll into Hogwarts. While protecting Hermione from the troll attack, Harry accidentally stuck his wand up the troll's nose, covering it in troll bogies. Based on the description, slime makes the perfect consistency for troll bogies. Just be careful not to accidentally stick your wand in it!

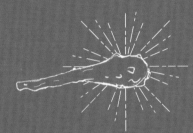

WHAT YOU WILL NEED:

- *Measuring cups, bowl, and spoon*

- *½ cup of Elmers® washable PVA clear glue*

- *1 cup of water, divided (½ to mix with glue and ½ [hot] to mix with borax powder)*

- *¼ tsp borax powder (You can find this in the laundry aisle)*

- *Green and brown gel food coloring*

- *Airtight container*

- *Jute twine (optional)*

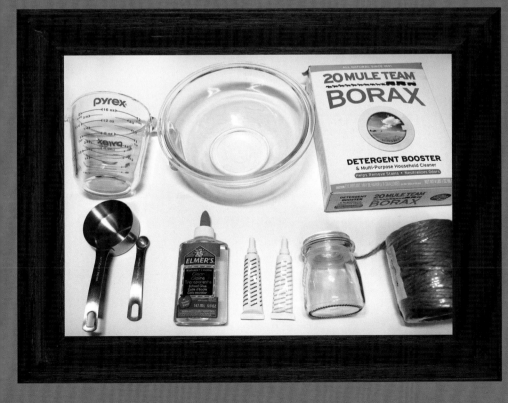

1. First, measure out ½ cup of the clear glue into a mixing bowl and then add your first ½ cup of water. Stir to combine.

2. Next, measure out ¼ tsp of borax powder and ½ cup of hot water (hot tap water is fine; it does not need to be boiled). Add the borax powder to the water and stir well to combine. This is your slime activator.

3. Add a few drops of your food coloring to the glue/water mixture and stir to combine (add more drops if you want a stronger color).

4. Then add your borax solution to the glue/water mixture. Start to stir—it will come together quickly! Keep stirring until your slime has formed then remove immediately. Knead the slime with your hands for several minutes to improve the consistency. (With the ratio of borax to water you should not have leftover liquid in the bowl.)

5. Once your slime is the perfect consistency, you can place it in an airtight container. (Slime in an airtight container can last for several weeks to several months if stored well!) I chose a glass jar with an airtight lid.

6. Then you can wrap twine around the neck of the bottle using the technique highlighted on page 3 to make it feel like a potion ingredient.

* Make sure to wash your hands thoroughly after playing with your slime.

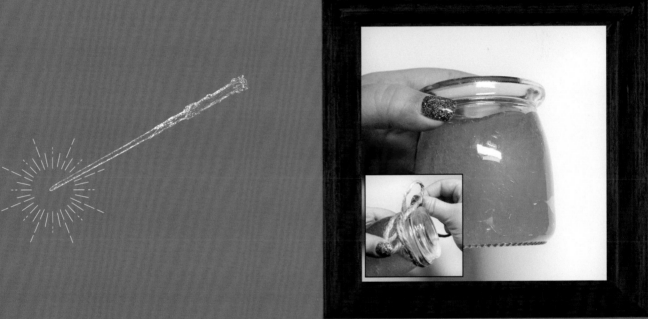

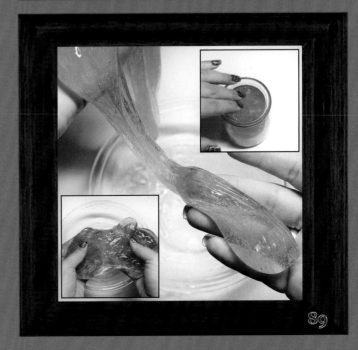

Harry Potter
Chocolate Frog Soap

One of the most popular Wizard Treats at Honeydukes is the Chocolate Frog. Each Chocolate Frog comes with a famous witch or wizard collectible card, and are able to jump and act like a frog because they are made of seventy percent Croakoa. Now you can learn how to make a Chocolate Frog Soap that will leave a chocolaty scent and have germs hopping away!

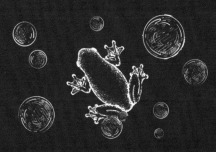

WHAT YOU WILL NEED:

- 4 ounces goat's milk melt-and-pour soap base

- 1 ounce raw cocoa butter (I used unrefined because it has a stronger cocoa smell)

- Glycerin

- 1 tablespoon cocoa powder

- Heat-resistant glass measuring cup (I use Pyrex®)

- Plastic spoon

- Chocolate soap fragrance oil (optional—you really don't need this unless you want a really strong scent).

- Small spray bottle filled with rubbing alcohol

- Frog molds (chocolate and soap molds work the same)

1. Take your four ounces of goat's milk melt-and-pour soap base and one ounce of unrefined cocoa butter and place them in a heat resistant container. Melt them in the microwave in thirty-second intervals, stirring in between each interval, until completely melted.

2. While you are melting your soap base, mix the glycerin into the cocoa powder until it starts to have a melted chocolate consistency. (It will clump at first and act like it isn't taking any moisture on; keep slowly adding the glycerin and mixing until it finally starts to combine.)

3. Once both compounds are ready, pour your cocoa into the melted soap base and whisk until thoroughly combined. (If you want a stronger chocolate scent, add the chocolate soap fragrance oil.)

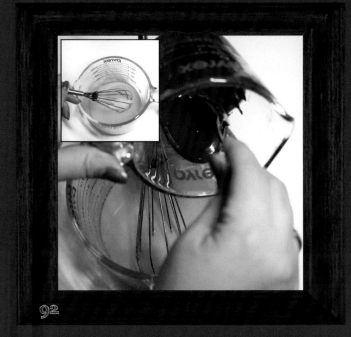

4. Spritz your mold with a fine mist of rubbing alcohol. This will help the soap come out of the mold much easier.

5. Once your mold is sprayed, fill each cavity to the top with the chocolate soap mixture. Then spray another spritz of the alcohol on top of the soap to keep bubbles from forming.

6. Allow your soap to dry at room temperature. If placed in the refrigerator it can make the soap chalky while it dries. I let mine dry overnight, but it should be dry within four to five hours.

7. Once your soap is dry, turn your mold over and flex it back and forth to loosen the soap and then carefully tap the mold to relaease the soap.

8. Once your soap has come out of the mold, it is ready to use and will leave your skin smooth from the cocoa butter and with a slight chocolate scent.

Harry Potter

Skele-Gro

Skele-Gro is a dreadful-tasting potion that is able to mend broken bones and even regrow bones that have been lost. Re-growing bones is a slow and very painful process that can take over twenty-four hours. Skele-Gro is usually bought in Diagon Alley but can also be brewed with great care. Store-bought Skele-Gro comes in a large skeleton-shaped bottle, and now you can make your own Skele-Gro bottle for your potion shelf!

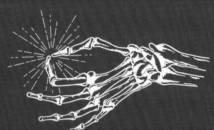

WHAT YOU WILL NEED:

- *Glass bottle*

- *Skull (foam or plastic, whatever feels right proportionately)*

- *Hot glue gun*

- *White paint (acrylic, craft, or spray paint)*

- *Black paint (acrylic, craft, or spray paint)*

- *Paintbrush*

- *Cooking skewer*

- *Skeleton arms (from plastic skeleton)*

- *Potion label printed on sticker paper (or regular paper and glue)*

1. First, paint your glass bottle with white paint (you can use acrylic paint like I did, or you could use spray paint or craft paint).

2. Then pull the arms off of your plastic skeleton. Once you have removed the arms, dry brush some of your white paint. You still want to see the details so don't solid paint them.

3. Let your bottle and arms dry completely. If need be, give your bottle a second coat to completely cover it.

4. Once your bottle is dry and completely covered take some black acrylic paint and dry brush or dab with a rag so you can add some aging and match the skull more closely.

5. If your skull is foam like mine was, press it onto your bottle where you want to glue it. It should leave an indent from the top of the bottle. Take a cooking skewer and press that indent in deeper so it leaves a path for the hot glue.

6. Now, line the indent with your hot glue and stick your head to the top of the bottle.

7. Once your skull is in place, glue your arms onto the bottle to make it look like a skeleton.

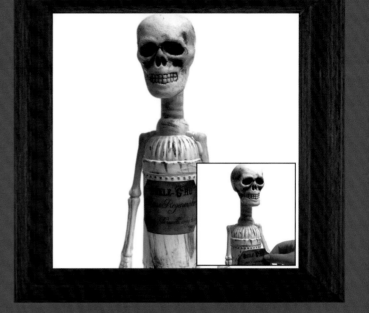

8. After your glue has cooled, take your white paint and cover any glue that is showing so it blends in with your bottle. Then dry brush some of the white onto the skull so the color of the head and body feel as one.

9. Finally, after all of the paint has dried, apply your label. If you are using the sticker paper you can just peel the backing and place it on the bottle. If you are using regular paper you can apply your label with glue or Mod Podge®.

 To see me make this Skele-gro Bottle, scan this QR code!

Essence of Dittany

Dittany is a magical plant with powerful healing and restorative properties. When Essence of Dittany is applied to a wound, the wound is healed at an increased rate, causing green smoke to billow upward. The skin regrows over the wound, making it look as if it has been healed for several days, preventing scarring. A few drops alone are enough to heal large wounds.

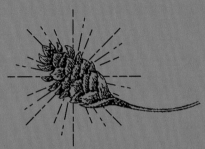

WHAT YOU WILL NEED:

- *Amber/brown glass bottle with a dropper*

- *Funnel*

- *Rubbing alcohol*

- *Metallic acrylic paint (I used bright gold)*

- *Potion label printed on sticker paper (or regular paper and glue)*

- *Lighter*

- *Gold chain*

- *Pliers*

- *Tiger-eye crystal charms or other charms*

- *Extra jump ring*

- *Jute twine (optional)*

How to make it

1. First, unscrew the dropper of your bottle and remove. Then use your funnel to fill the bottle with rubbing alcohol.

2. Once your bottle is filled, pour some of your gold metallic paint into the rubbing alcohol.

3. Screw the cap back on and shake until the paint is completely mixed into the alcohol and you get a great swirling effect.

4. Take your label, either printed on sticker paper or regular paper and carefully, and use a lighter to burn the edges. I recommend doing this outside. Be ready to blow the flame out pretty quickly, so you don't overburn the edges. (If you have a Cricut you could have it cut a faux burn look and go around the outside edge with a brown marker to mimic the burn effect.)

5. Take your gold chain, measure out the length you want, and cut to size with the pliers. Then open up the end jump ring and attach your charm. In this case I used a tiger-eye crystal charm. When you are done both ends of the chain should have a charm.

6. Take an extra jump ring and use it to wrap the chain around the neck of the bottle. (It looks better to have your ends hang uneven rather than even.)

7. Once your chain and charms are in place, stick or glue your label onto the bottle.

8. To give a more complex look you can wrap the base of the dropper with jute twine. (See page 3, Wrapping the Neck of Your Bottle.) You can also use your lighter to carefully "age" the twine.

To download this Essence of Dittany Potion Label scan this QR code!

To see me make this Essence of Dittany Potion Bottle scan this QR code!

Harry Potter
Unicorn Blood

Unicorn blood has the appearance of a thick, shimmery silver substance. The blood of a unicorn can be drunk to keep a person alive even if they are nearly dead. However, the act of slaying a unicorn will cause the drinker to suffer a cursed life, which is why the sale of Unicorn Blood is strictly forbidden and controlled by the Ministry of Magic. Quirinus Quirrell drank Unicorn blood on Voldemort's behalf, since they were sharing a body, in order to sustain Voldemort's life.

WHAT YOU WILL NEED:

- *Clear alcohol-free thick styling gel*

- *Disposable piping bag (or a sandwich bag with the corner snipped off)*

- *Silver acrylic paint*

- *Silver glitter*

- *Spoon for mixing*

- *Glass bottle with cork*

- *Potion label printed on sticker paper (or regular paper and glue)*

- *Jute twine (optional)*

- *Lighter to age twine (optional)*

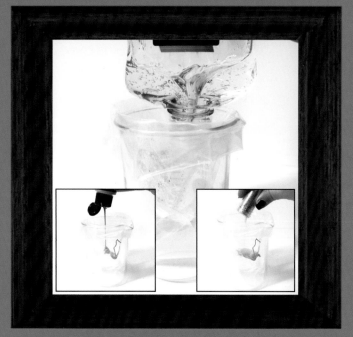

How to make it

1. Place your piping bag or sandwich bag inside a cup or vase and fill it with a little bit of hair gel—you don't want the bottle filled all the way up.

2. Once you have your gel in the piping bag add some silver acrylic paint and silver glitter. Mix thoroughly with a spoon until you get the color and sparkle you want.

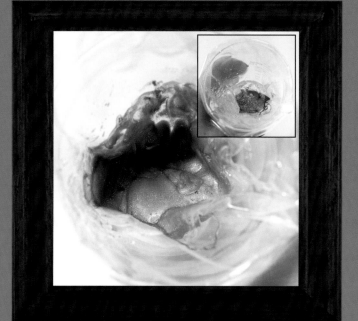

3. After your "unicorn blood" is ready, pull your piping bag out of the cup and cut the end with scissors. Insert the end of the piping bag into the bottle and fill the bottle with the gel.

4. As soon as your bottle is filled, if you want more "sparkle" to your solution, sprinkle some more glitter onto the top of the gel. Once you are satisfied re-cork the bottle.

5. With your bottle re-corked you can place the label on the bottle. If you are using sticker paper remove the backing and stick it to the bottle (otherwise use regular paper and glue).

6. To give a more complex look you can wrap the neck of the bottle with jute twine. (See page 3, Wrapping the Neck of Your Bottle.) You can then "age" your twine by carefully using a lighter to darken the twine.

 To see me make Unicorn Blood Bottle scan this QR code!

Cornish Pixie Lantern

A Cornish Pixie is a small, bright blue magical creature that loves wreaking havoc. These small, flying troublemakers are incredibly strong creatures considering their size; they can easily lift a human into a tree! If your Pixies are set loose, they can be rounded up with a freezing charm, *Immobulus!* After you have caught your pixies you can keep them locked up in this lantern.

WHAT YOU WILL NEED:

- *Lantern*

- *Frosted glass spray paint (I recommend Krylon®)*

- *Cornish pixie silhouettes cut out of vinyl or regular paper*

- *LED light (I purchased mine from Harbor Freight)*

- *Blue permanent marker*

1. Remove the glass from your lantern: usually there are tabs on the inside that hold the glass. Open the tabs and carefully remove the glass.

2. Once the glass is removed lay it out on some newspaper or cardboard. Using the Krylon frosted glass spray paint, spray thin even coats onto the glass. Wait one minute or more between coats. I applied six coats.Once your glass is sprayed, allow it to dry for at least an hour before handling them.

3. After your glass is dry, apply your pixies to the non-sprayed side. If you are using vinyl, either hand cut or cut by a Cricut. You will want to use contact paper to help apply them. If you are using sticker paper or regular paper simply stick them on with the adhesive or with glue.

4. After you have applied your pixies to the unsprayed side of the glass reinsert the glass into the lantern the same way you pulled it out.

5. Take your LED light and color it in blue. This will make the light from the lantern blue. (If you ever want to remove the blue simply wipe it off with some rubbing alcohol.)

6. Once your lantern is back together place your light in the base of the lantern and re-latch it. You have captured your Cornish pixies!

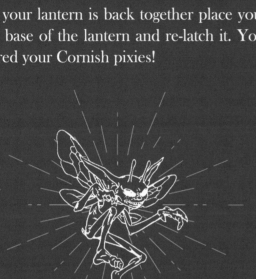

To download the Pixie Design scan this QR code!

Harry Potter

Acceptance Letter

Hogwarts Acceptance Letters are sent to all magical children in the UK once they turn eleven years of age, even those who are muggle-born. The letters are written on parchment paper and sealed with a red sealing wax bearing the Hogwarts Crest. All letters are delivered to the recipient by owl except in the case of muggle-borns. Their acceptance letters are delivered in person by a member of the Hogwarts faculty. If your Hogwarts Acceptance Letter never made it, now you can make your own!

WHAT YOU WILL NEED:

- *2 sheets of 8.5" x 11" parchment-looking paper*

- *Printer or copy shop*

- *11" x 17" ivory paper (also called tabloid size)*

- *Scissors (or a Cricut® machine)*

- *Glue stick (I prefer the kind that goes on purple and dries clear)*

- *Hot glue gun*

- *Red hot glue or sealing wax*

- *Hogwarts crest wax seal stamp (you can use a button, etc., if you do not have one, or don't want to buy one.)*

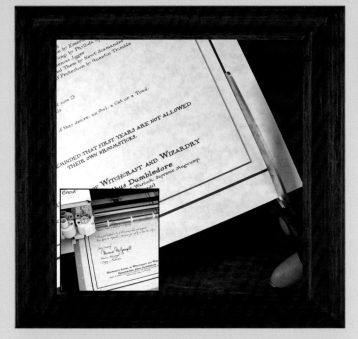

How to make it

1. First, you will need to personalize your letter and print it, or you can print Harry's. (The actual letter and supply list are smaller than 8½" x 11" so they can be printed on standard letter-sized paper. If possible, print on a parchment-looking paper).

2. Next, you will need to personalize the envelope or, again, print Harry's. Then you will need to have it printed at a copy shop, unless you have a large format printer. The size of the paper needed for the envelope is 11"x17", or tabloid size.

3. Once all of your pages are printed, cut them out. This can either be done with scissors or a Cricut machine. (If you are cutting the letter pages with a Cricut you will use the "print then cut" setting.)

4. Fold your envelope. Use the glue stick to glue together where the sides overlap. (Be sure to put a piece of scrap paper into the envelope before gluing so, you don't accidentally glue it to the back of the envelope.)

5. Glue the bottom flap up and press firmly to make sure you have good adhesion.

6. While your envelope is drying fold your acceptance letter and supply sheet in half.

7. Once your envelope is dry, slip your letter inside and tack your top flap down with a glue stick.

8. Then use your hot glue gun or sealing wax to pool some of your red glue or wax onto the edge of the top flap of your envelope. While it is still hot press your wax seal stamp (or button) into the glue or wax. Let your stamp sit there for a minute while it cools, then remove the stamp.

* If you are mailing your letter (via US Postal Service), one stamp should suffice.

 To download the Letter Template scan this QR code!

Harry Potter
Golden Egg Bath Bomb

The Golden Egg was the goal of the first task of the Triwizard Tournament. The eggs contained a song sung by merpeople, letting the Triwizard Champions know that they had to come to the black lake and rescue something very valuable to them. Merfolk cannot sing above water, so the song could only be understood while under water. If opened on land, the egg would screech and make a horrible racket. Now you can make magic in your tub with your own Golden Egg—just be sure to release it in water!

WHAT YOU WILL NEED:

- *2 bowls for mixing*

- *¼ cup cornstarch*

- *¼ epsom salt*

- *½ cup baking soda*

- *¼ cup citric acid*

- *Whisk and spoon*

- *1 tsp carrier oil (coconut, castor oil, and almond oil are best)*

- *½ tsp essential oil (I used a tangerine-scented oil)*

- *½ tsp water*

- *Yellow food coloring or soap coloring*

- *Plastic Easter eggs (larger ones work best. Use rubbing alcohol to clean them)*

- *Gold spray food coloring*

How to make it

1. After dumping all of the dry ingredients (cornstarch, epsom salt, baking soda, citric acid) into the bowl, whisk them together. Continue mixing until all of the ingredients are well incorporated and there are no lumps.

2. Now mix the wet ingredients (carrier oil [I used castor oil], essential oil, water, food coloring) in a separate bowl.

3. Then *slowly* add a drop or two of your wet ingredients into the dry ingredients at a time, whisking the whole time. If you do not continually whisk and add the wet in gradually, the wet will activate the dry ingredients and it will start to fizz and your bath bomb will continue to foam up instead of dry out.

4. Continue to combine the ingredients and continue mixing until it looks like fresh powdered snow; it should start to stick together when you pinch it. (If it feels too wet, or sounds like it is fizzing, add more of your dry ingredients to balance it back out).

5. Now that your dry and wet ingredients are mixed, you can take your egg mold and start to scoop and press your mixture into both halves of the mold. Press the bath bomb mixture firmly into the mold with the back of a spoon.

6. Once your egg is filled and pressed you can mound some more of the mixture on each side. Then press your two halves together until they are packed tightly together.

7. Allow your bath bombs to dry at least four hours or overnight. Once you are ready to unmold your bath bomb tap on the plastic to help detatch the mold from the bath bomb egg. Carefully lift the egg halves off of your egg bath bomb.

8. You are then left with a light yellow, fragrant Golden Egg Bath Bomb. To help it look more golden use your gold spray food coloring (I used Wilton) to cover your egg. The spray food coloring is light enough that it doesn't get your egg wet enough to activate it.

9. When it is placed in the water it fizzes beautifully, leaving your water a magical yellow gold color with a refreshing tangerine scent!

* These make a great gift!

Harry Potter
Peruvian Instant Darkness Powder

Peruvian Instant Darkness Powder is sold at Weasley's Wizard Wheezes in Diagon Alley as part of their defensive products. It is an imported magical item that creates darkness when used, allowing the user to be unseen while escaping. As its name indicates, it was invented by the wizarding community in Peru. The Darkness Powder is purchased as a dark, glittery, multicolored rock. Now you can have your own supply of the darkness powder!

WHAT YOU WILL NEED:

- *Lava rocks*

- *Black flash, blue flash, gold metallic, and blue metallic acrylic paint*

- *Black extreme glitter paint or Mod Podge®*

- *Black fine glitter, iridescent black fine glitter, black regular glitter*

- *Glass cylinder bottle with cork*

- *Labels printed on sticker paper or regular paper and glue*

1. Start by taking your lava rock and painting it completely with the black flash acrylic paint with a paintbrush, pressing the bristles into all of the crevices of the rock.

2. Then take the blue flash, blue metallic, and gold acrylic paint and sporadically blend the colors into the rock, mimicking an "oil slick" look.

3. Let the paint dry completely. Then take the extreme black glitter paint and add some of the iridescent black and standard black extra fine glitter, as well as some standard size black glitter, and mix it in together. (If you don't have the extreme glitter paint use Mod Podge and all of the glitter.)

4. After making the glitter paint mixture, paint your rock completely and allow it to dry completely. If you want more glitter add a second coat.

5. While your Peruvian Instant Darkness Powder dries, take your glass cylinder bottle and apply your label. If you are using sticker paper simply apply the label to the bottle. (If you are not using sticker paper you can use regular paper and Mod Podge or glue.)

6. Then add your star label to the top of the cork to complete the look of the jar. Then fill your jar with some of your completed Peruvian Instant Darkness Powder.

* You can also wrap a piece of the Darkness Powder with gold mylar and tie it like a gift.

 To download the Labels scan this QR code!

 To see me make the Peruvian Instant Darkness Powder scan this QR code!

Hocus Pocus
Life Potion

Winifred Sanderson and her two younger sisters, Mary and Sarah, lived in a cottage on the outskirts of Salem in the late 1600s. As they started to age, Winifred used her spell book to find the perfect potion to keep them young and beautiful forever! The Life Potion elixir allows the brewer to suck the drinker's life-force away in order to replenish their own youth and vitality. The potion works best on young children, as they have the most youth to transfer. The more children the Sanderson Sisters manage to drain, the longer they shall live, until they become immortal.

WHAT YOU WILL NEED:

- *Glass bottle with cork*
- *Sandpaper*
- *Frosted glass spray paint*
- *Compressed air*
- *Green dish soap*
- *Green food coloring (if your green soap is not dark enough)*
- *Cup*
- *Spoon*
- *Piping bag*
- *Tag printed on tan paper*
- *Scissors*
- *Jute twine*
- *Brown marker*
- *Lighter*

1. First, take your glass bottle and use the sandpaper to rough it up and give it an aged look.

2. Once your bottle looks aged on the outside, take your frosted glass spray paint and spray it into the neck of the bottle. This will give your bottle a smoky look, since the life potion has a steamy smoke.

3. To assist with the drying of the frosted spray paint, you can use the compressed air to speed up the process. Otherwise it may take a couple hours to dry.

4. While the inside of your bottle dries take your green dish soap and add it to your cup. Then add some green food coloring to get your desired green color. (you may not need to add any depending on the color of your dish soap).

5. Load your dish soap into a piping bag or a plastic sandwich bag and snip the corner. Place the bag into the neck of the bottle to help fill it without getting your bottle messy, then re-cork your bottle.

6. Once your bottle is filled, it is essentially done, but you can take it a little further by adding a tag. Print your tag on brown or tan paper so that it will appear more aged. (You can cut a brown paper bag to 8.5" x 11" and load it into your printer if you don't want to buy brown paper.) Then cut it out and punch a hole in the top. To add aging to the tag, go around the outside edges with a brown marker

7. Use your jute twine to tie your tag onto your bottle. Once your tag is tied twist the twine in the opposite direction it is wound; this will unravel the individual strands. You can then "age" your twine by carefully using a lighter to darken the twine. (Light your cord and blow it out; your twine will smolder slowly.)

Free download of the Life Potion Tag. Or visit: https://cookingandcraftchi.wixsite.com/mysite

To see me make this Potion Bottle scan this QR code!

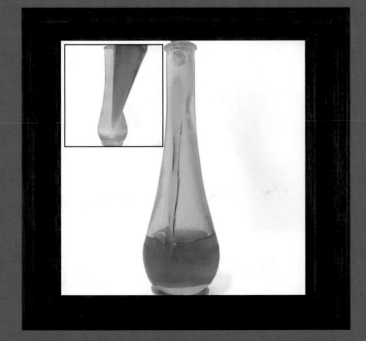

125

Hocus Pocus
Black Flame Candle

Made from the fat of a hanged man, the Black Flame Candle produces a black flame composed of dark fire. As written and explained in the Sanderson Sisters' spell book, the candle, if lit by a virgin on All Hallows' Eve during a full moon, would raise the Sanderson Sisters from the grave for as long as the flame burned, which was one night only.

WHAT YOU WILL NEED:

* *LED pillar candle, or regular pillar candle (at least 6" tall and has to have a wax coating on the outside)*

* *Design printed on tissue paper in the same color as the candle*

* *Packing tape*

* *Copy paper*

* *Wax paper*

* *Heat Gun or hair dryer*

* *Black permanent marker*

* *Scissors*

* *X-ACTO® knife (optional)*

1. Start by cutting your matching tissue paper (ivory tissue for an ivory candle, white for white, etc.) to a little smaller than a sheet of copy paper. Use the packing tape to tape the tissue paper to the copy paper (I like for the smoother side of the tissue to be face up). Then print the design on the paper. (Make sure your front edge is taped down smooth and half of the tape is wrapped around to the back so the printer won't jam.)

2. Once your design is printed on the tissue, use scissors to cut the tape off, freeing the tissue paper.

3. Wrap and position the tissue around the candle, with the printed side facing up. If your paper is taller than the candle it is okay; you can cut the excess off later.

4. After you have the tissue design wrapped, take a sheet of wax paper that is longer than your candle and hold the tissue in place. Be sure that your tissue didn't move and everything is in place—this is the last chance you have to adjust the placement.

5. Now that the wax paper is wrapped take your heat gun or hair dryer and start to move the heat up and down the candle. (Avoid holding the heat on the same spot for too long, so the candle doesn't become misshapen.) You will start to see the design darken trough the wax paper—this is the design setting into the candle. Continue to heat the design until the whole design shows through.

6. After the design is transferred, carefully peel the wax paper back revealing your newly designed candle.

7. If you did have any excess tissue above the edge of your candle use an X-ACTO knife to trim it away. Once it is trimmed away use the heat gun briefly to watch that edge disappear.

8. Now you need to color the flame black (if you are using a real candle you will omit this step). Use your permanent marker to color the flame. Light it up and you have a Black Flame Candle!

 To download the Black Flame Candle design scan this QR code!

The Legend of Zelda
Medicinal Potions

These potions are medicinal drinks with magical properties in The Legend of Zelda series. They can heal Link, refill his Magic Meter, or both, as well as have other unique effects. The most common potions are the Red, Green, and Blue Potions, as they perform the most basic and relevant behaviors to Link. The Red Potion is the Medicine of Life and replenishes his Health. The Green Potion is the Medicine of Magic and restores Link's Magic Bar. The Blue Potion is the jack-of-all-trades, Medicine of Life and Magic, or the Cure-All Medicine.

WHAT YOU WILL NEED:

- *Piping bags*

- *Clear alcohol-free thick styling gel*

- *Red, green, and blue food coloring*

- *3 bottles with corks*

- *Labels printed on sticker paper (or regular paper and glue or Mod Podge®)*

1. Place your piping bag or sandwich bag inside a cup or vase and fill it with a decent amount of hair gel—enough to fill your bottle all the way up.

2. Then add your food coloring to the gel. Mix thoroughly, being sure to fold the gel all the way to the bottom to make sure all of the gel is the same color.

3. Once you have your desired color, mix the other two colors so you have three piping bags filled with the red, green, and blue gel for our potions.

4. Take your piping bag and squeeze all of the gel to the bottom, and then snip the end so you can fill your bottle. Place the piping bag into the uncorked bottle and fill it to the top with your colored gel. Do this with all three colors and all three bottles.

5. Once your bottles are filled, recork your bottles.

6. Now you can apply your potion label to the outside of the bottle. If your bottle feels like it has a film, use some rubbing alcohol on a paper towel to clean the bottle. If you are using sticker paper, simply remove the backing paper and stick the label to the bottle. (On curved bottles you may need to use your nail or a credit card to rub the edges down thoroughly.) If you are not using sticker paper you can use regular paper and glue or Mod Podge to stick it to the bottle.

7. Once you have applied your label to your bottles they are complete. If your bottle will be around children you may want to glue the cork onto the bottle. I recommend using E6000 glue to glue the cork on.

To download the Potion Labels scan this QR code!

The Lord of the Rings
Gandalf's Fireworks

Gandalf the Grey was well-known in the Shire for his amazing fireworks and firework shows. Gandalf created many different kinds of fireworks, namely "squibs, crackers, backarappers, sparklers, torches, dwarf candles, elf-fountains, goblin-barkers and thunder-claps."[*] He also created fireworks shaped as objects like stars, trees, or dragons. This is a great recycling project—you can use used paper towel and toilet paper tubes, as well as old mail tubes, and even used tissue paper or wrapping paper. Get creative and see what you have laying around that can become a magical firework prop.

WHAT YOU WILL NEED:

- *Paper tubes of all sizes*
- *Tissue paper in fun colors*
- *Card stock in fun colors*
- *Tape*
- *Woven place mats or burlap, etc. (anything with some texture)*
- *Rope or twine*
- *Wooden dowels*
- *Ribbon*
- *Hot glue gun and glue*

---

* Tolkien, J.R.R. *The Fellowship of the Ring.* Houghton Mifflin Harcourt, 2012. Chapter 1.

1. First, begin by wrapping your tubes in tissue paper.

2. You may want to make some as groupings of fire-works, or twist the ends to look like a fuse. You may want to add little cones to the top to look like a rock-et firework. To do this, cut circles out of your card stock and make a slit halfway through and glue it into a cone, then attach it to the tube.

3. Use items like woven place mats, burlap, etc. to wrap larger tubes to give them a unique textured look.

4. Bundle some of the tubes together and wrap them with ribbon or twine.

5. You may decide to glue a dowel to the bottom of the tubes to look like the part that would stick in the ground. Don't forget to add some twine fuses too.

* Have fun with this—you can make any type of firework you want. You could even re-wrap existing fireworks or sparklers to really put on a show at a party!

Encantus Spellbook

The Encantus is Merlin's magical textbook that teaches both magic and spells. An Encantus magically records the art, history, and science of sorcery (including both past and present struggles between benevolent Merlineans and wicked Morganians). There have been many copies of the Encantus given to many conjurers, including those on both sides. Now you can have your own copy of the spellbook!

WHAT YOU WILL NEED:

- *An old book (I purchased mine at a library sale)*

- *Merlin's circle printed on copy paper*

- *Pencil*

- *Gold paint marker*

- *Gold metal book or page corners*

- *Pliers and a cloth*

1. Make sure that you have a nice old book, with as little print or no print on it at all. If you can't find a plain book you can decoupage a new cover on it with tissue paper and Mod Podge®. Just ensure it is completely dry before moving on to the next step.

2. Take your printed Merlin Circle and flip it over. On the back of the sheet use the edge of the pencil to fill it in. (Make sure that your pencil is dark enough to give a nice dark transfer.)

3. Flip your design back over and place it where you would like it on the book. Once you have it in place, trace over the design. Be sure to press hard and make your lines thick enough.

4. When you remove your paper, you will have a pencil transfer on the book that you can follow with your gold paint marker. Do your best to keep your lines a consistent width.

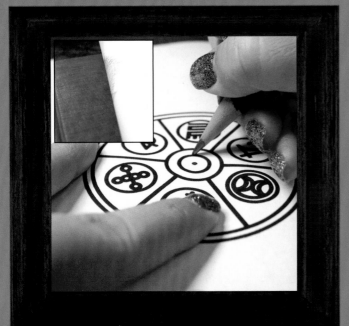

5. After your design is drawn on, place your metal book corners onto the corner of the spellbook. Pinch the corner on tightly with a pair of pliers. (Be sure to cover the front, ornate portion of the corner with a cloth to protect it from getting scratched by the pliers.)

6. Once all of the corners are placed on the book your Encantus is complete.

 To download Merlin's Circle Design scan this QR code!

The Chronicles of Narnia
White Witch's Ice Wand

The White Witch's wand was an implement of great but terrible dark magic. It was owned by the White Witch, who used it to win control over Narnia in the Winter Revolution and maintain power during her reign. While the true extent of the wand's capabilities was unknown, its signature power was the ability to turn organic matter into stone, and the only thing that could undo such a curse was the breath of Aslan. Now you can have a light-up, unbroken Ice Wand—unlike the genuine artifact which was shattered by Edmund's sword at the battle of Beruna.

WHAT YOU WILL NEED:

- *Chopstick or dowel rod*

- *Pearl-colored acrylic paint*

- *Foam brush*

- *Floralyte (floral LED light)*

- *Hot glue gun*

- *Hot glue (I used extra-strength glue sticks for this)*

1. First, you will need to paint your chopstick with the pearl acrylic paint and foam brush. Allow it to dry completely before moving on to the next step.

2. Once your wand is dry, hot glue the Floralyte LED light to the end of the wand (if there is any text on it, try to glue that side to the wand so the white side is facing out).

3. Once your light is secure, test that you can pull and push the on/off switch without it coming off of the wand.

4. After the light is secured, take your hot glue gun and begin covering the light, building up the area around it so that it looks like one smooth, cohesive piece. (You may need to wait a few minutes for each layer to cool so that the additional hot glue doesn't keep melting the under layers and will actually build up rather than keep melting.)

5. Continue to cover the rest of the wand with the hot glue, making sure to go back and forth to keep the glue textured. This will give it more of an ice appearance.

6. As you drip and apply the glue to the wand, taper it to a rounded point so it appears to look like an icicle. (Again, you may need to let the layers cool completely in between applications to get the icy look we are going for.)

7. Finally, allow your wand to cool and pull the on/off tab to illuminate your icicle wand!

* This is the perfect accessory to our White Witch's Ice Crown (p. 147)!

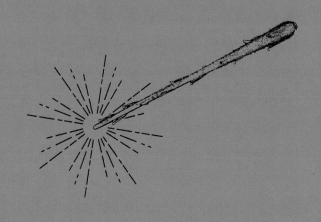

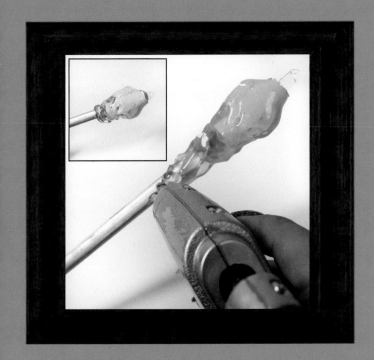

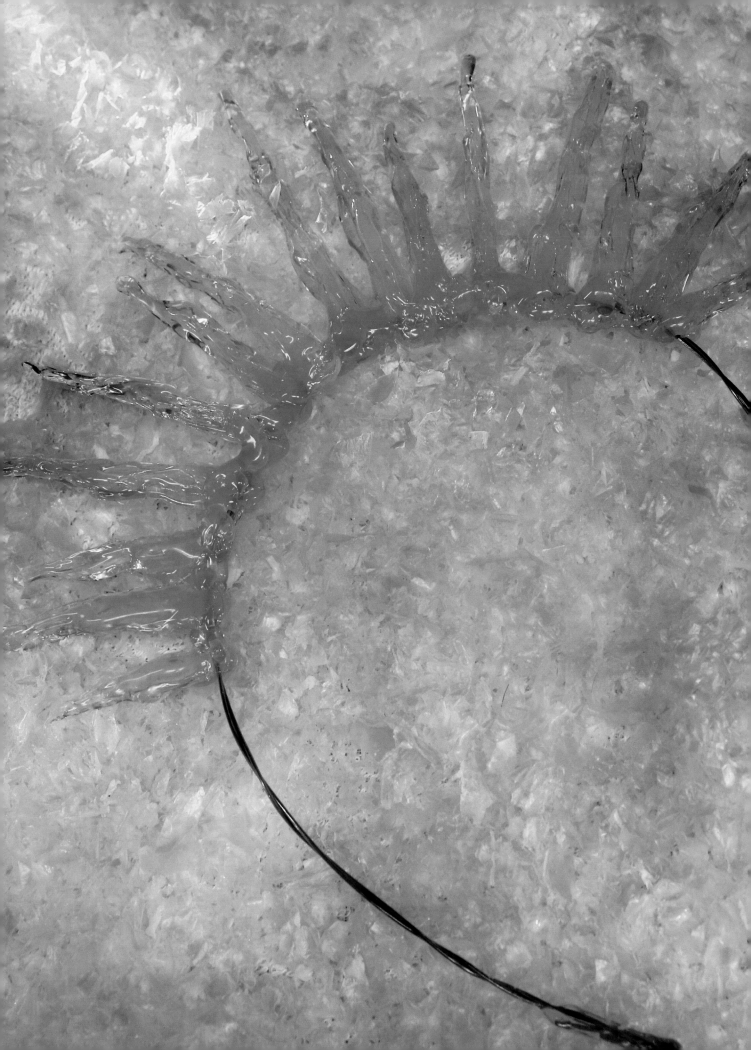

The Chronicles of Narnia
White Witch's Ice Crown

Queen Jadis the White Witch of Narnia laid a curse upon her Narnian subjects, beginning the Long Winter, which magically forced Narnia into a hundred-year state of frozen snow and ice. The winter lasted all through her reign, thus earning her the title of the White Witch. Now you can have her Ice Crown to go with her Ice Wand!

WHAT YOU WILL NEED:

- *2 pieces of silver floral wire*

- *Pliers*

- *Hot glue gun*

- *Hot glue (I used extra-strength glue sticks for this)*

- *Glass surface to glue on, like a baking pan, a window, etc. (I used a 9 x 13" glass baking pan)*

1. Start by taking your two pieces of floral wire and twisting them together to create a thicker wire for your headband.

2. Once your wire is twisted, shape the wire into the upside-down U shape of a headband. When you have your desired shape bend the bottom of each side of wire up and crimp it with pliers.

3. After your wire is crimped, use the hot glue to coat the bottom of the wire so it stays together, and won't get caught in your hair when you are wearing it.

4. Then you can begin forming your icicles for your crown. Start by laying down your glass surface and start to draw icicle lines on it with the hot glue gun. (I use the extra-strength glue sticks to make sure the icicles won't bend and flop over.) Once you have drawn your different sized "icicles" and they have completely cooled, peel them off your glass surface.

5. When you have all of your icicles you can lay them face down on your glass surface in the pattern you would like your crown to take on.

6. Once you have them laid out the way you would like, lay your wire headband on top, and start to connect the headband to the icicles with the hot glue gun.

7. After one layer is complete continue to build your icicles up so they are connected to the headband and start to take on a more three-dimensional look.

8. After you are satisfied that the icicles are all attached and built up, go through the space between the icicles and add more glue to cover the wire at the top of the headband crown.

*   Let your crown completely cool and wear your Ice Crown!

Shakespeare's Macbeth
Witch's Brew

The Three Witches, also known as the Weird Sisters or Wayward Sisters, are characters in William Shakespeare's play *Macbeth*. These witches set a tone for all future witches in fiction. This is their Witch's Brew!

"Double, double, toil and trouble; / Fire burn, and cauldron bubble!" (*Macbeth* IV.i.10–11)

WHAT YOU WILL NEED:

* *Mist maker/fogger/water atomizer with LEDs*

* *Water*

* *Vase or cup that is shorter than the cauldron but taller than the mister*

* *Cauldron of any kind (preferably waterproof)*

* We are going to give our "Witch's Brew" a bubbly potion effect without the use of dry ice (in other words, without the cost, danger, or hassle). To achieve this you will need to get a mist maker/fogger, which is a water atomizer. These are around $10 or less and you can use them for several things besides a witches brew: they can make a jack-o'-lantern fog from its opening, take an outdoor fountain or pond to a whole new level, or even make bath time interesting! The beautiful part about the fogger is it's reusable and safe for kids and adults to touch—unlike dry ice.

1. First, place the fogger into the glass container, and fill it with water. It is important not to submerge your fogger too deep or it won't work; however, if your water doesn't completely cover it, it won't work either.

2. Once your fogger is in the water, place your container into your cauldron. Be aware that these foggers can splatter water, so make sure that you either place your cauldron outside or on a surface that is ok to get wet.

3. Then plug your fogger in and voila, you have great color from its LED lights and flowing fog. This makes a super magical effect—just make sure you have extra water nearby to keep your container full.

** I use these foggers every year for Halloween in my pumpkins and cauldrons and they mesmerize kids. They all ask if it's real witch's brew!

Sleeping Beauty

Sleeping Beauty

Maleficent's Staff

Maleficent is pure evil, a villain who will do whatever it takes to achieve her goals. In Disney's *Sleeping Beauty* (1959), she is frequently accompanied by her pet raven, Diablo, and she carries a staff with a glowing green orb at the tip.

Using her staff, she can conjure up her spells like lightning projection, divination, and teleportation. She can even cast powerful dark magic spells like her forest of thorns. Her powers also make her capable of shapeshifting at will into numerous forms, including a floating hypnotic light and a massive, monstrous, black and purple dragon!

WHAT YOU WILL NEED:

- *Glass or plastic clear ornament bulb*
- *Pledge® Floor Care Finish*
- *Cup to empty ornament*
- *Green glitter*
- *Mini LED light (often found in the foral section)*
- *Hot glue*
- *Craft foam*
- *Scissors*
- *Floral wire*
- *Gold paint*
- *Large wooden dowel*
- *Gold ribbon*

1. Start by taking your ornament bulb and filling it with some of the floor polish. Swirl the polish around so the entire inside of the bulb is covered. Dump the excess polish out and leave your bulb to sit upside down to completely drain and to allow the polish to get tacky on the inside.

2. Once your bulb has sat for a few minutes, add your green glitter to the inside (I recommend the extra fine glitter). Then swirl the glitter around your bulb until it is completely covered. Again, dump the excess glitter out of the bulb. Let it sit and dry before moving onto the next step.

3. After your bulb has dried, take your LED lights and add some stuffing or some tissue around them, anything that will help diffuse the light.

4. Push the lights up into the bulb and hot glue your battery pack to the bulb so they can't come out.

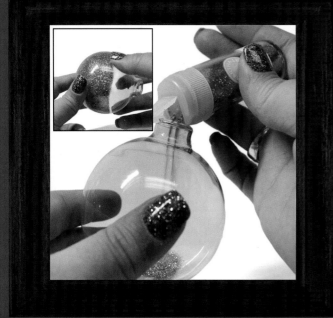

5. Next, take your craft foam and cut out a leaf shape. Use your first cut-out as a template to make seven more so you have eight identical leaves total. Now take your floral wire and glue it to one of the leaves, then add more glue and sandwich two leaves together. Trim any excess wire, and now your leaf is bendable.

6. After all of your leaves are wired, paint them gold (unless you used gold craft foam).

7. While your leaves dry, paint your entire dowel gold. After your staff has dried, glue your light-up bulb to the top.

8. Now you can glue your four leaves around the bulb, bending and shaping them to contour away from the bulb.

9. After your leaves are glued on, glue one end of your gold ribbon to the back and wrap your ribbon to cover up the connection point for your leaves. Glue it closed and your staff is complete.

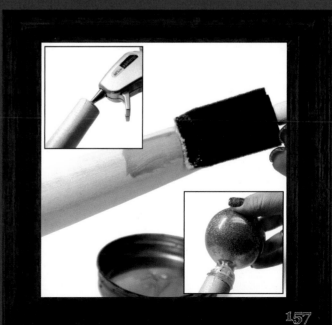

Snow White and the Seven Dwarfs
Poison Apple

The blood-red Poisoned Apple was prepared by The Evil Queen Grimhilde. Once the magic apple was bitten, it would send its victim into the Sleeping Death, which could only be reversed by love's first kiss. To make the apple the witch brewed the potion in her cauldron and dipped an ordinary apple into it, allowing the brew to seep into the apple. Once complete she raised the apple from the cauldron allowing it to reveal the evil within, portrayed as a dripping skull image.

WHAT YOU WILL NEED:

- *Fake red apple*
- *Permanent marker*
- *Glue gun*
- *Black hot glue*

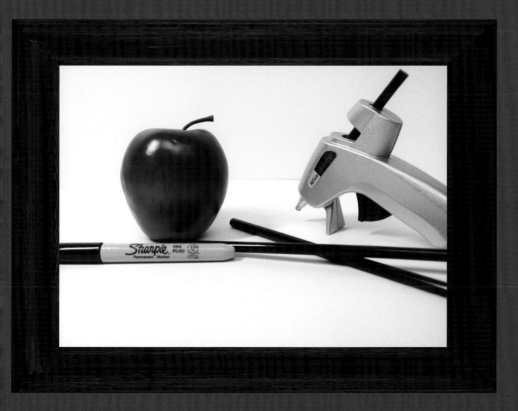

1. First, take your fake apple and draw a skull eyes and nose shape with a permanent marker. You will use these outlines as a guide for your hot glue.

2. Next, take your black hot glue and draw over the lines you drew. Allow these to cool completely before continuing, because these lines need to act as a dam that prevents the dripping glue from going into the skull details.

3. Once those have cooled, start at the bottom and randomly drip your glue, giving the illusion of the poison dripping off of the apple. Again, allow this to cool before adding more layers.

4. Continue adding drips in layers all the way around the apple. (Be careful not to glue your stem down while you are adding the black hot glue.)

5. Once you have your desired look, allow your apple to cool completely. If you want more drips, continue to add layers of the hot glue to the apple.

* If your drips are not dripping enough, you can use a heat gun or hair dryer to help the process.

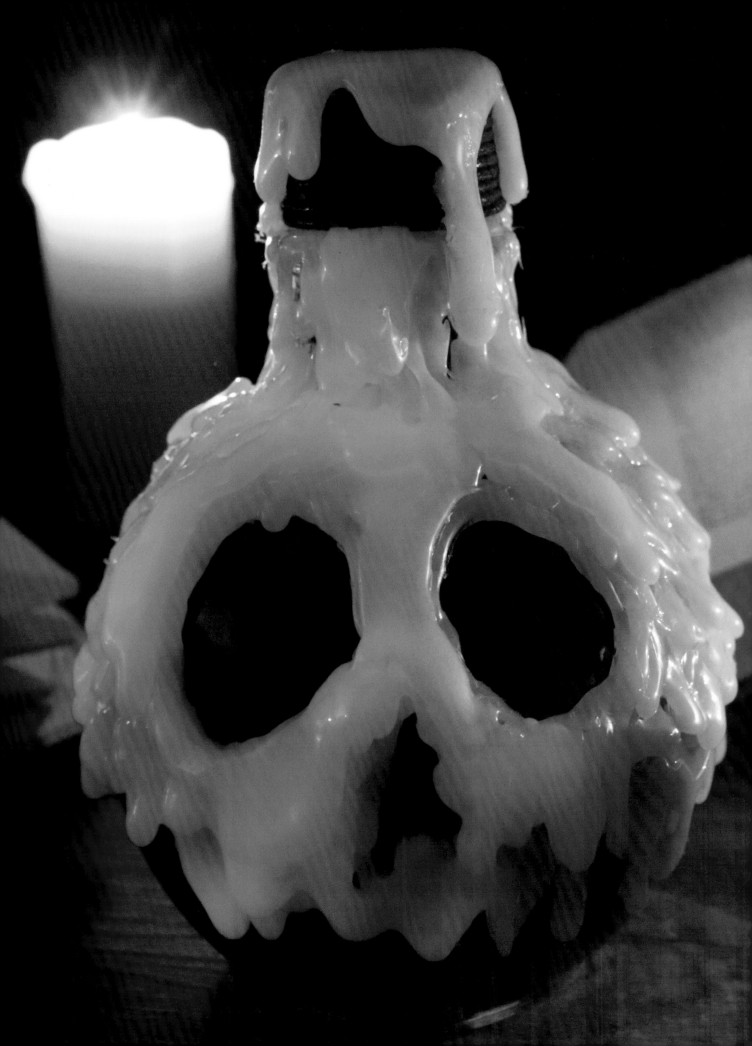

Snow White and the Seven Dwarfs
Death Apple Potion

The Evil Queen Grimhilde obsessed over being the fairest in the land, a title that was held by her beautiful stepdaughter, Princess Snow White. In her desperation she uses her spell book and cauldron to mix a potion that transforms her into an old witch to disguise her from Snow White. Then she conjures another potion, a poison to taint an apple, which will cause the princess to fall into a cursed, death-like slumber. This is the vessel to hold the Evil Queen Grimhilde's Death Apple Potion. This is a perfect prop for a Snow White fan, or a Halloween or cosplay costume.

WHAT YOU WILL NEED:

- *Round glass bottle*

- *Rubbing alcohol*

- *Black permanent marker (optional)*

- *Chalk marker or dry-erase or wet-erase markers*

- *Hot glue gun*

- *Glow-in-the-dark hot glue (on this size bottle, I used about 2 packs of the glue)*

- *Black metallic paint (I used FolkArt® Color Shift Black)*

- *Black cording*

1. Wipe the entire bottle down with rubbing alcohol to ensure that there is no dirt or a film on the bottle.

2. If the cap of your bottle is not black, color it in with a permanent marker so it will camouflage behind your cording.

3. Use a chalk marker or a wet or dry erase marker to draw the outline of the skull eyes and nose. Make sure to use a removable marker so any excess can be wiped off.

4. Then use your hot glue gun loaded with the glow-in-the-dark hot glue to trace the lines we created. Be sure to build the glue up decently so it will act as a barrier against the dripped hot glue.

5. Start to use your hot glue gun to drip the glue to create a drippy texture all around the bottle. Make sure not to let the glue drip in the eye or nose holes.

6. Once you have covered your bottle with the dripped hot glue fill your bottle with rubbing alcohol.

7. After your bottle is completely filled, add your black metallic acrylic paint. It is important that your paint is metallic so that it will give your "potion" a swirling effect when shaken or swirled around

8. Re-tighten your cap and shake your bottle until the paint is completely mixed in with the rubbing alcohol.

9. Use your black cording to wrap around your cap to cover it completely. (Use the diagram on page 3 to see how to wrap your cap without glue.)

10. To complete your bottle, drip more glue on the top of the cap to conceal it. Let the glue drip down over some of the cording so it incorporates into the rest of the bottle. Turn out the lights and enjoy the glow of your Death Apple Potion.

To see me make this Potion Bottle scan this QR code!

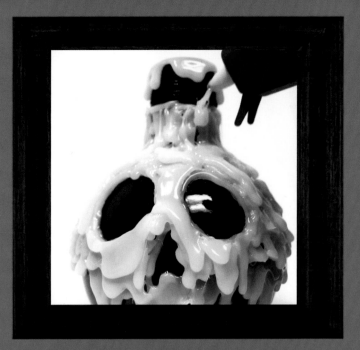

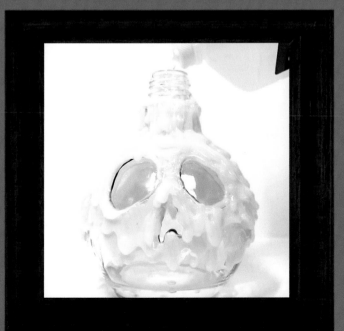

Tangled
Magical
Golden Flower

A long time ago, a single drop of sunlight fell from the heavens to the ground, and a beautiful golden flower grew. It had the ability to heal any sickness or wound, as well as keep one young forever. However, for the flower to have the ability to delay aging it required regular enchantments to preserve its power. Mother Gothel discovered the golden, glittery flower and its abilities, and used it for centuries until it was finally discovered and uprooted, its powers eventually being transferred to the Princess Rapunzel.

WHAT YOU WILL NEED:

- *Artificial yellow lily*

- *Zig® glue pen*

- *Purple extra-fine glitter*

- *Floral wire and gold floral tape, or gold wire*

- *Pliers*

- *Hot glue gun and glue*

- *LED fairy lights strand*

- *Round wooden base (I used a clock base so it had a hole pre-drilled in the center)*

- *Moss*

- *Glass dome or cloche*

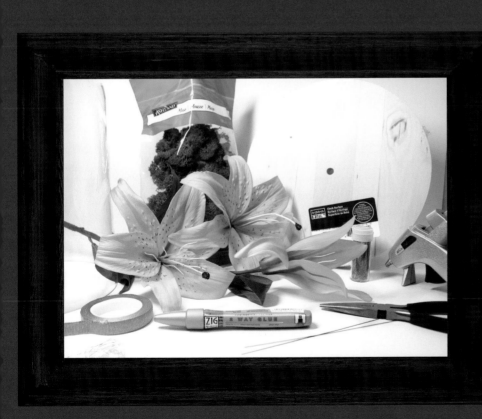

How to make it

1. Start by trimming your lily to the height it needs to be to fit under the dome, as well as trimming any excess flowers off the stem.

2. Now take your Zig glue pen and draw a curly design on the inner portion of your petals, and sprinkle the purple glitter over the glue. Dump off/blow off any excess glitter.

3. While your glue is drying, take your floral wire and wrap it with the gold floral tape (or use gold wire). Then take your pliers and wrap the wire around them, creating a curly swirl for the center of the flower. You will make three of these.

4. Now that you have your curled wire you will hot glue them to the center stamen of the lily. Once they are glued you can bend and form them how you want around the center of the flower.

5. Once your lily has been glittered, begin wrapping the stem and base of the flower with your fairy lights. You want the light to shine through the petals and down the stem. Be sure to leave some extra lights to swirl loosely around the flower in the cloche too.

6. After you have lit your flower, take your hot glue and glue the base of the stem into the hole of your wood base, securing it in place.

7. Then cover the base of the stem with some moss. Start by adding some hot glue to the wood base and place your moss; this way it won't be able to move or shift when the cloche is lifted.

8. Now that your base has been mossed, carefully cover your flower, excess lights, and the moss with the glass dome, centering it on the wood base. Now you have your own Magical Golden Flower!

Evil Sea Queen Ursula's

Mermaid
to
Human
Potion

Poor Unfortunate Souls Apothecary

Ursula's Mermaid-to-Human Potion

Ursula is a villainous sea witch who "helps" unfortunate mermaids and mermen achieve their goals. She was banished from Atlantica by her longstanding rival, King Triton. Ursula sought vengeance by scheming to take hold of Triton's throne and therefore seize control of the ocean as Queen. Ursula finds that one of King Triton's daughters, Ariel, has fallen in love with a human prince named Eric, and sees her opportunity to take the kingdom. Ursula proposes an agreement where she will transform Ariel into a human for three days, during which Ariel must receive the "kiss of true love" from Eric. If Ariel succeeds her transformation into a human will be permanent, but if she fails, she will turn back into a mermaid and be bound to Ursula for eternity! This is the potion Ursula brews to transform Ariel.

WHAT YOU WILL NEED:

- *Spiral shell, moon shell, or shark eye shell*

- *Paintbrush*

- *Gold metallic acrylic paint*

- *Funnel*

- *Glass bottle with cork*

- *Rubbing alcohol*

- *Purple metallic acrylic paint (FolkArt Color Shift® Purple)*

- *Jute twine*

- *Hot glue gun and gold hot glue (or regular hot glue and a gold paint marker)*

- *Battery-operated LED light (I used one with mini lights)*

- *Potion label printed on sticker paper (or regular paper and glue)*

How to make it

1. First, take your shell and paint it with the metallic gold acrylic paint. (Don't paint it so solid that you can't see the features of the shell.)

2. While your shell is drying, use your funnel to fill your glass bottle with the rubbing alcohol.

3. Once your bottle is filled add your purple Color Shift paint (or a metallic purple of your choosing, but you need a metallic paint to get the swirling effect in your bottle), recork your bottle, and shake it up. (You may need to add more paint to get the desired color.)

4. After you have your desired color, use your jute twine to wrap the neck of the bottle. (To learn how to wrap the bottle without glue, see the diagram on page 3.)

5. Once the neck of the bottle is wrapped, use your hot glue gun to add drips around the top of the bottle and your cording. (If you do not have gold hot glue you can use regular hot glue and a gold paint marker to get a similar effect.)

6. Take your painted shell and insert your LED lights, making sure to keep the mechanism that turns it off and on accessible.

7. Now glue your shell to the top of the cork, again making sure that your LED light on/off switch is accessible. Then cover all but the switch with your glue to hide the mechanics.

8. Lastly, apply your potion label to the front of your bottle. Then you can shake or swirl your bottle and watch your potion swirl!

Free download of the Mermaid-to-Human Label or visit: https://cookingandcraftchi.wixsite.com/mysite

To see me make this Potion scan this QR code!

The Little Mermaid
Ursula's Voice Necklace

In order for Ursula to turn Ariel into a human, she asks Ariel for her voice, claiming that men only want silent women. Secretly, this is actually to ensure that Eric won't be able to recognize her. Ariel agrees and signs a contract. Ursula commands Ariel to sing and summons a pair of hands from her magic cauldron which slowly approach Ariel. As she sings, the hands rip her voice from her throat, silencing it, and placing it inside the necklace, causing it to glow!

WHAT YOU WILL NEED:

- *Spiral shell, moon shell, or shark eye shell*

- *Gold metallic acrylic paint*

- *Foam brush*

- *Black cording*

- *Battery-operated LED light (I used a Floralyte)*

- *Hot glue gun and glue*

1. First, take your shell and paint it with the metallic gold acrylic paint. (Don't paint it so solid that you can't see the features of the shell).

2. While your shell is drying, take your black cording and decide how long you want your necklace to be. I recommend that you make it long enough to go over your head, unless you want to add a clasp.

3. Once your shell is completely dry, take your battery-operated LED light and turn it on, then decide how you would like your light, or "voice," to be positioned. After you have decided the appropriate spot take your hot glue gun, add a drop of glue to the light, and adhere it to the shell. (For a more permanent placement of the light I would recommend using an E6000 glue.)

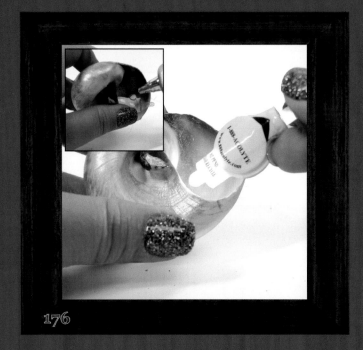

4. Once you have your "voice" light glued into place, glue your string onto the shell. I glued one side into the spiral of the shell and the other on the inside. I used hot glue but if you are using this for cosplay I would again use E6000 Glue. (You could drill holes into your shell, but you always run the risk of breaking the shell while drilling the hole.)

5. Once your twine is glued in place you can turn your light on and have a magical voice necklace just like Ursula's.

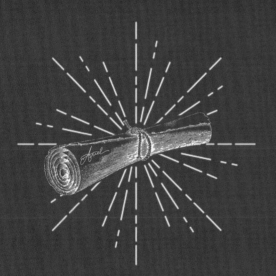

Snake
Venom

Witch's Ingredients
Snake Venom

Snake venom has long had a tradition of being part of witches' ingredients to various poisons, potions, and brews. The three witches in Shakespeare's *Macbeth* used snake venom in their brew, and even Voldemort from the Harry Potter series implemented his snake Nagini's venom to keep himself alive.

WHAT YOU WILL NEED:

- *Toy snakes*

- *Acrylic black paint*

- *Glass bottle with lid or cork (I used a recycled salad dressing bottle)*

- *Mod Podge®*

- *Paper towel that looks scaly*

- *Metallic taupe acrylic paint*

- *Foam brush*

- *Hot glue gun and glue*

- *Label printed on sticker paper (or regular paper and glue)*

- *Jute twine (optional)*

1. Start by painting your toy snakes black (I picked my pack of snakes up at the dollar store). Your snakes may need two coats of paint.

2. While your snakes are drying, coat your bottle with a healthy coat of Mod Podge. Then place your paper towel around the bottle tightly, using the Mod Podge to help hold it down. Trim any excess paper towel. Once your paper towel is roughly in place, start painting the Mod Podge on top of the paper towel, decoupaging the paper towel onto the bottle so it appears as a scaly texture. After you have completely covered your paper towel and are satisfied with your bottle, let it dry completely. This may take a few hours (I recommend letting it sit overnight).

3. Once your bottle is dry, take your metallic taupe or gold paint and dry brush over the texture on the bottle. This will give it an almost cloth or scale-like effect. Allow it to dry completely.

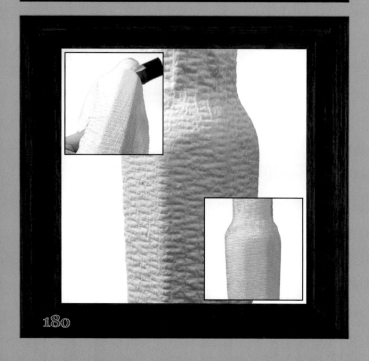

4. Now that your bottle is dry you can start to glue your snakes onto the bottle. Make sure they wrap around the bottle, giving it movement and dimension.

5. After your snakes have been applied to the bottle you can apply your potion label. If you are using sticker paper simply remove the backing paper and stick it in place. If you are using regular paper and Mod Podge coat the back and place it on the bottle. Cap or cork your bottle and your snake venom is complete!

* Depending on what your lid looks like, you may want to wrap the top with jute cording (see Wrapping the Neck of Your Bottle on page 3).

 Free download of the Snake Venom Label. Or visit: https://cookingandcraftchi.wixsite.com/mysite

Pure & Superior Quality

Toad Warts

Boil or Fry for 10 Minutes

Witch's Ingredients
Toad Warts

Toad parts, especially the warts, have long had a tradition of being part of witches' ingredients to various potions and brews. Even the three witches in Shakespeare's *Macbeth* used a toad in their brew. J. K. Rowling even wrote about toads and their importance in witchcraft throughout the Dark Ages, saying, "a British toad could think itself lucky if it died of natural causes, because it was in constant danger of being boiled, powdered, skinned or tied around a sick human's neck in a bag."*

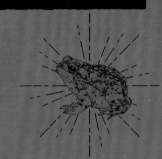

WHAT YOU WILL NEED:

- Glass surface to glue on (I used a glass baking pan)
- Moss
- Hot glue gun with glue
- Green and brown permanent marker
- Cup and spoon for mixing
- Clear alcohol-free thick styling gel
- Neon green and brown food coloring
- Disposable piping bag (or sandwich bag with the corner snipped off)
- Glass bottle with cork
- Cooking skewer
- Label printed on sticker paper (or regular paper and glue)
- Jute twine (optional)

* Rowling, J. K. "Toads by J. K. Rowling." Pottermore. Pottermore Limited. 2019. https://www.pottermore.com/writing-by-jk-rowling/toads.

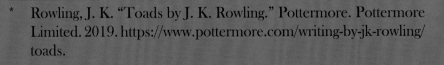

How to make it

1. First, take your glass surface and make sure it is flat so it's easy to glue on. Then ball up some small pieces of moss so they are a good size for the center of the warts.

2. Next, use your hot glue gun to enclose the ball of moss. Continue to do this until you have a good number of "warts" to place in your bottle.

3. Once the "warts" are cool, you can pop them off of your glass surface.

4. To make the warts show up more in the styling gel, use permanent brown and green markers to color them.

5. After the "warts" are complete, fill your cup with clear styling gel. (The thickness of the gel creates a great suspension quality.) Then add a little neon green and brown food coloring and mix until you get the desired color.

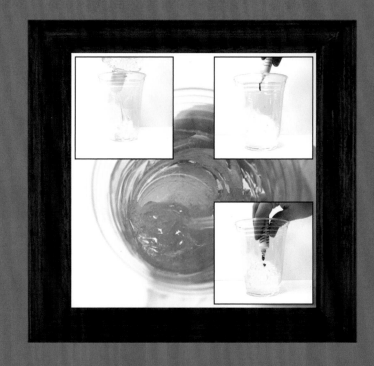

184

6. Once you have the desired color, fill your piping bag with the styling gel. Cut the end of the bag off and pipe some of your gel into the bottle. (Don't fill it all the way up until you get most of your warts in the solution.)

7. Start to place your warts into the gel, using the cooking skewer to help you position the warts throughout the bottle. After all of the warts are in the bottle fill it to the top with the rest of the gel.

8. After the bottle is filled re-cork the bottle. Then you can place the label on the bottle. If you are using sticker paper remove the backing and stick it to the bottle. (otherwise use regular paper and glue).

9. Finally, embellish the bottle with some of the moss and a jute twine tie (optional).

Free download of the Toad Warts Label. Or visit: https://cookingandcraftchi.wixsite.com/mysite

To see me make these Toad Warts scan this QR code!

Witch's Tools
Crystal Ball

A crystal ball, also known as an orbuculum, is used as a common fortune-telling object, usually being associated with clairvoyance and scrying. They are used often by many media representations of witches and wizards, from the Wicked Witch of the West in *The Wizard of Oz* to Jareth the Goblin King in *Labyrinth* to Sybil Trelawney in the Harry Potter series. Now you will have the ability to make your own crystal ball so you can look into the future!

WHAT YOU WILL NEED:

- *Fiber fill (pillow stuffing)*

- *Black spray paint*

- *Terrarium base with glass globe*

- *Purple fairy lights*

1. First, lay some of the fiber fill out on some cardboard or newspaper. From a far distance, lightly mist the fiber fill with the black spray paint to give your fiber fill a "smoky" effect. *Please spray paint in a well-ventilated area under adult supervision.

2. After your fiber fill has dried, start to fill your glass orb with the fiber fill. Be sure to show a variation of the smoky grey and white filling. Press the filling around the edge leaving the center hollow.

3. Once your glass orb is filled and has a hollow center ,take your fairy lights and unravel them. (If your lights are not purple you can use a permanent marker to color the lights to your desired color.) With your lights unraveled start to fill the hollowed out center with your fairy lights.

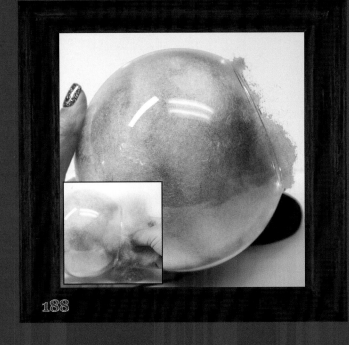

4. Once your lights are all placed into the fiber fill add more fill to finish completely filling your crystal ball. Then place your ball on top of the wood base. (You can either tuck the battery pack up into the ball or you can string the cord out of the back of the crystal ball.)

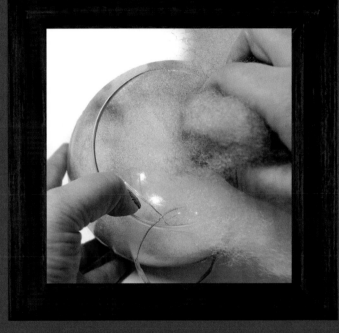

Witch's Broom

Witches have been illustrated riding the popular cleaning tool well before the silver screen depicted the Wicked Witch of the West or Harry Potter taking flight. Ever since the fifteenth century the broomstick has been intricately bound with the image of the witch. Widely believed to be the witch's favorite mode of transport, the broomstick serves as both vehicle and tool. Now you can make your own broom to soar across the sky!

WHAT YOU WILL NEED:

- *Dried grass or thin twigs*

- *Scissors or floral trimmers*

- *Stick/branch for the handle*

- *Zip ties*

- *Hot glue gun and glue*

- *Jute twine*

How to make it

1. First, take your dried grass or twigs (I used prairie grass) and, if needed, trim it to an appropriate length

2. After all of your broom base is trimmed, lay it out evenly and you can either discard the base of your grass or save it for a smaller broom.

3. Once it is laid out slip the two zip ties under the broom base. Then lay your stick/branch handle on top.

4. Start to gather your broom base around the handle as you pull your zip tie closed. Once one zip tie is completely secure, pull the second one. After both zip ties are on your broom, make sure that they are pulled as tight as you can get them.

5. Place the bumped up zip tie closures together and to the side or back of your broomstick.

6. Now you can trim your zip ties to the closure. Then, because the closures bump up slightly, use your hot glue to help smooth them out so you can wrap your twine more easily.

7. Now you can wrap your broom using the wrap method for the neck of our potion bottles shown on page 3. This wrap method will let you wrap your broom without gluing or knotting your twine.

8. Once you have wrapped your broom with the twine trim any long ends. Now you have a beautifully customized broom. You can make it as big or as small as you would like and you can get creative by wrapping ribbon or gluing flowers or any other decorations to your broom.

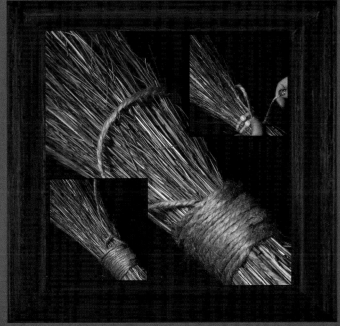

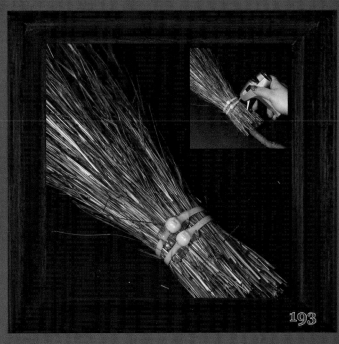

The Wizard of Oz
Glinda's Wand

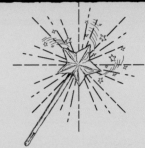

After the Wicked Witch of the South was vanquished, the Good Witch of the North and ruler of Quadling County, Glinda, became known as Glinda the Good. Glinda is beautiful, educated, independent, and wise, and because of all of these qualities she is the most respected sorceress in all of Oz. Glinda was depicted in all pink and sparkles in the 1939 cinematic feature of *The Wizard of Oz*, where she helped country girl Dorothy get back to Kansas. Now you can use this affordable wand to help you get to Oz!

WHAT YOU WILL NEED:

- *Chopstick or small dowel*
- *X-ACTO® knife*
- *Silver acrylic paint*
- *Foam brush*
- *Scissors*
- *Light pink glittery scrapbook card stock, cut into 2 star shapes*
- *Mod Podge® or glue*
- *Iridescent rhinestones*
- *Light pink vellum cut into 2 smaller stars*

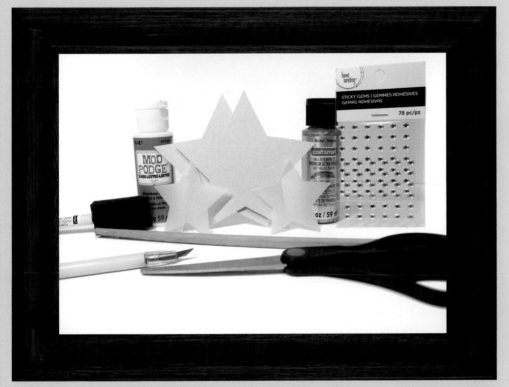

How to make it

1. Start by taking your X-ACTO knife and carefully making a slit in the top of your chopstick (this is where your large star will be inserted). I made my slit about a half an inch deep.

2. Then paint your chopstick/wand handle silver with your acrylic paint. (Allow it to dry completely before inserting your star.)

3. Take your glittery card stock and either hand cut it into a star, or have a Cricut® cut it. To hand cut it evenly you can print a large star and a small star on copy paper, cut it out, and trace the star on the back of the paper to give you a guide to cut on.

4. After your stars are cut out Mod Podge or glue the entire back of the star and stick both sides together so your star is glittery on both sides. (You may need to press it under a book while it dries, because the card stock may want to curl.)

5. Once your large star has dried place some of your adhesive iridescent rhinestones on each corner.

6. Then you need to cut your light pink vellum into two smaller stars. (Again, either hand cut it into a star, or have a Cricut cut it. To hand cut it evenly use the small star printed on copy paper, cut it out, and trace the star on the back of the vellum to give you a guide to cut on.)

7. After your stars are cut out go all the way around the edge of the star with iridescent rhinestones and then do a rhinestone in the center as well as five surrounding stones to fill it in.

8. Now, because your vellum stars will sit higher than the large star because of the chopstick, flip your star over and use hot glue to build the back up so it will lay flat.

9. Finally, insert your large star into the slit in the wand we made (if loose add a drop of hot glue) then glue your smaller vellum stars to both sides of the wand and you have an inexpensive Glinda Wand!

The Wizard of Oz
Wicked Witch's Hat

The Wicked Witch of the West is quite possibly the most iconic depiction of a Witch ever shown on the silver screen. In MGM's 1939 *The Wizard of Oz*, the Wicked Witch of the West has a flawlessly evil look, with green skin, a black dress, a broom, and a pointy black hat. Ever since the Wicked Witch of the West was shown in the conical hat with a wide brim, it set a precedent for witches in popular culture. Now you can have the Witch's Hat to wear yourself.

WHAT YOU WILL NEED:

- Chalk, or a silver permanent marker

- String

- 1 yard heavy felt

- Ruler

- Scissors

- Hot glue gun and glue

- Large black satin ribbon

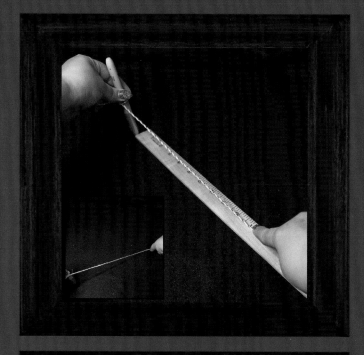

* This hat should fit most adults and some kids.

1. First, take your piece of chalk or permanent marker and tie it to a piece of string that is at least 26" long. This is the tool we will use to get the perfect circles for the base of the hat.

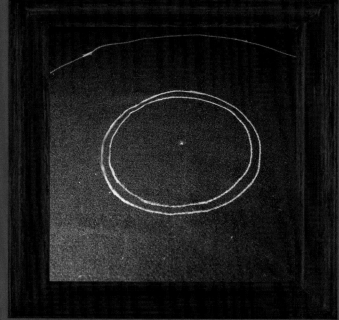

2. Now, lay out your felt and take your chalk with string and measure your string to 10". Hold the string down on your fabric at the 10" mark and draw a circle on your felt, like a big protractor. Use your chalk to make a mark where you were just holding your string down (this is the center of your brim). Then measure your string to 4"; again, hold the string down in the center of your brim and make a smaller circle inside of your larger circle (this is where your head goes or the crown). Measure your string one more time to 3½" and draw one more circle. This is the area where we are going to glue the cone to the brim of the hat.

3. Once your brim is drawn, cut out the outside of the brim circle and the inside of the smallest crown circle. Then cut out little tabs in the inside curve of the brim circle to, but not past, our 4" line.

. Now we are going to measure our cone for the hat. Lay your felt out flat and measure 25¼" from the left edge and make a mark. Then measure up from that mark 19" and make another mark. Measure 12⅝" to the left from your 19" mark—this is now your top point. Using a yard stick, draw a line from your 25¼" points to the top point (this should form the sides of your cone). Then measure your chalk and string to 19", hold the string down to the top point, and draw a curve starting at the bottom left edge going to the bottom right edge. Then add a ½" flap onto one of the sides of your cone—this is where you are going to glue it down. Cut the entire cone shape out, including the flap you drew.

5. Now it is time to assemble: fold your hat cone in half and hot glue the flap down to finish the crown. (Glue sections at a time, holding the flap down as your glue cools.) Place your cone on the table standing up and bring your brim down over the top of the cone until it is lying on the table. Glue the little tabs from the brim down around the base of the cone. Once your glue has dried, flip it over and finish gluing the brim to the cone.

5. Again, once your glue has cooled flip it back over right side up and tie your large satin ribbon around the base of the cone leaving ribbon tails flowing behind. (If your ribbon is satin you can carefully take a lighter and melt the end of the ribbon so it won't fray.)

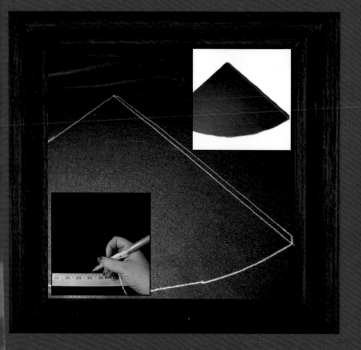